Lives of Notable
Asian Americans

THE ASIAN AMERICAN EXPERIENCE

Lives of Notable
Asian Americans

ARTS ❀ ENTERTAINMENT ❀ SPORTS

Geraldine Gan

EDITORIAL CONSULTANT: RONALD TAKAKI
PROFESSOR OF ETHNIC STUDIES
AT THE UNIVERSITY OF CALIFORNIA, BERKELEY

Chelsea House Publishers

New York ❀ Philadelphia

On the cover : Kristi Yamaguchi, Zubin Mehta, and Maya Lin.

Chelsea House Publishers

EDITORIAL DIRECTOR   Richard Rennert
EXECUTIVE MANAGING EDITOR   Karyn Gullen Browne
COPY CHIEF   Robin James
PICTURE EDITOR   Adrian G. Allen
ART DIRECTOR   Robert Mitchell
MANUFACTURING DIRECTOR   Gerald Levine
ASSISTANT ART DIRECTOR   Joan Ferrigno

The Asian American Experience

SENIOR EDITOR   Jake Goldberg
SERIES DESIGN   Marjorie Zaum

Staff for *Lives Of Notable Asian Americans:
Arts * Entertainment * Sports*

EDITORIAL ASSISTANT   Scott D. Briggs
PICTURE RESEARCHER   Pat Burns

First Printing

1   3   5   7   9   8   6   4   2

Library of Congress Cataloging-in-Publication Data
Gan, Geraldine.

Lives of notable Asian Americans: arts, entertainment, sports/
Geraldine Gan.
p. cm. — (The Asian American experience)
Includes bibliographical references and index.
ISBN 0-7910-2188-2.
I. Asian Americans—Biography—Juvenile literature.
[I. Asian Americans—Biography.] I. Title. II. Series: Asian American
experience (New York, N.Y.)
E184.06G36 1995   94–26812
920'.009295073—dc20
    [B]   CIP
                                                   AC

Contents

Michael Chang displays the winning trophy after defeating Stefan Edberg of Sweden in the men's singles final of the 1989 French Open tennis championship.

MICHAEL CHANG IS ONE OF AMERICA'S TOP TENNIS PLAY-
ers. In 1989, at age 17, he was the youngest player ever to
rank in the top five in the world. Throughout his career, he
has won matches over such tennis greats as André Agassi,
Jimmy Connors, and Ivan Lendl. A debilitating hip injury
temporarily stalled his career after his 1989 French Open title,
but since his recovery Michael has been making a steady
comeback to the top, performing competitively in all subsequent Grand Slam tournaments he has entered.

Michael Chang was born on February 22, 1972, in
Hoboken, New Jersey. He has one brother, Carl, who is three
years older. Michael's father, Joe Chang, a research chemist
for Unocal, was born in Canton, China. After the revolution
in China in 1949, Joe and his family moved to Taiwan, and
in 1966 Joe immigrated to the United States on a student visa.
He was pursuing a master's degree in chemistry at the Stevens
Institute of Technology in Hoboken when he met Michael's
mother, Betty Tung, who was born in New Delhi, India. She
came to the United States at age 11, when her father, a
diplomat for the Republic of China, became a consular offi-
cial at the United Nations. Betty and Joe first met in New
York on a blind date.

They married, and in 1974, after they had their two
sons, the Chang family moved to St. Paul, Minnesota, where
Joe took a job with the 3M company and Betty attended the
University of Minnesota, eventually graduating with a degree
in medical technology. Joe took up tennis that year, and it
quickly became his obsession. He read books and magazines
to improve his knowledge of the sport and spent all his free
time on the courts. Betty suggested that Joe take his sons
along, and in 1978 Joe introduced Michael and Carl to the

Michael
Chang

sport of tennis. The Chang mythology has it that six-year-old Michael learned the rudiments of the game by standing on a chair at a Ping-Pong table in the basement of the Changs' house in St. Paul.

A year later Joe moved his family to La Costa, in southern California, so the Chang boys could play tennis year-round. A Chinese saying, which Betty later quoted in an interview, goes "Mung mu san tien"—"a mother will move many times for the sake of the child." Joe and Betty were willing to sacrifice a lot to develop their sons' tennis ability. Rather than enroll them in tennis camps and pay for expensive coaches, the Changs practiced in round-robin games as a family, playing every day of the week except Monday. On weekends the boys competed in local tennis tournaments. Michael won his first match in competition at age seven, in a tournament at San Diego's Balboa Park. Soon afterward he was nationally ranked for his age group, and it became clear that Michael would be the family tennis prodigy. Carl kept up his tennis, too, and eventually went on to play for the University of California at Berkeley.

Throughout Michael's training coaches were brought in on a temporary basis, including Phil Dent, Roy Emerson, Dennis Ralston, Jan Russell, José Higueras, Pancho Segura, and Brian Gottfried. But Joe Chang remained Michael's main coach. The others had too much ego, Joe believed, and only he had Michael's best interests at heart. He would sit in on Michael's lessons, watch other players' videos, and soak up a near-scientific knowledge of tennis, which he passed on to his son. He formulated graphs and flow charts monitoring Michael's progress. "Tennis is chemistry," he explained in a magazine interview. "Creating a tennis champion is 90%

information gathering and 10% creativity. The important thing is to have the right 90% of information." Michael enjoyed having his dad as a coach. As he explained to a reporter, "Something doesn't click when I go to other coaches. . . . No coach in the world is going to replace what my dad has done, how he has worked with me. . . . In my eyes, my dad will always be my coach."

Through periodic "family council" meetings, all the members of the Chang family keep closely involved in decisions about Michael's career, a practice which earned them their nickname of the "Chang Gang." Others in the tennis community have even gone so far as to call their close-knit nature "family bondage." There was pressure on him, but Michael accepted it. He felt that his family would always be there for him no matter what he did, and he was grateful.

When Michael was 12, the family decided to implement a plan for Michael's career. It was a decision requiring a lot of investment, and there was no turning back. In 1985 the Changs refinanced their home in La Costa to pay for Michael's training and travel costs on the juniors tennis circuit. Betty traveled with her son on weekend tennis matches. She acted as his support system on the road, preparing his meals, sewing his tennis shorts, and even stenciling the P on his Prince racket. In 1986, at age 14, Michael was the youngest player for the Junior Davis Cup team. In 1987, at 15, he became the youngest to win the USTA National juniors. Six months later he became the youngest male to compete in the U.S. Open at Flushing Meadow since Vinnie Richards in 1918.

When Michael beat Australian player Paul McNamee in four sets in the first round, the world began to take notice of Michael as the new rising American star among the current tennis champs, including Arthur Ashe, Jimmy Connors, and John McEnroe. Unlike them, however, Michael was only five feet eight inches, 131 pounds, and somewhat bowlegged. He got attention because, as he put it, he was "Fifteen and stuff," and "Chinese and stuff." He was known for being a nice, down-to-earth young man. That year he declined an invitation to try out for the Junior Davis Cup team again because he didn't want to "miss out" on being a teenager. "Life could get boring," he told a reporter.

The Changs moved to Placentia, California, in July of 1987, and life for Michael only got more interesting. In six weeks of playing four pro tournaments, his ATP ranking moved 800 points up, to No. 164. In February of 1988 he was offered a multi-million-dollar contract by the sportswear company Reebok. After getting his GED certificate in March, he quit high school and turned pro. Betty quit her job as a chemist to travel with him full time.

That summer, at 16, Michael became the youngest player on Wimbledon's Centre Court since 1927. In January 1989, he was the youngest to play on the U.S. Davis Cup team since 1928. In April he defeated the No. 1-seeded Ivan Lendl for the first time, in Atlanta, and by the time he traveled to Paris for the French Open the following month, he was ranked No. 18 in the world. Of the four Grand Slam events—the Australian Open, the French Open, Wimbledon, and the U.S. Open—the two-week-long French tournament is considered the most grueling. Because of the red clay surface on the courts at the Stade Roland Garros, which slows the ball after it bounces, a big serve is not as effective as on a hard court. Michael's French Open match depended less on his serve,

which was his weakness anyway, and more on endurance, precision, and strategy, his strengths.

In the French Open semifinal round Michael went up against Ivan Lendl, and Joe didn't think his son had a chance. Lendl won the first two sets, so Joe didn't bother to stay for the rest of the match. But Michael was able to gain the next two sets, tying the match at the fifth set. His legs began cramping, but he adjusted his strategy, lobbing the ball on his strokes, buying himself time to rest as he wore Lendl down trying to return them. At match point Lendl's first serve was long, and as a way to psych him out, Michael moved well inside the baseline, as if to say that he knew Lendl would blow the second serve too. Michael's strategy worked. Lendl dou-ble-faulted long, bumping Michael up to the quarterfinals, where he defeated Haiti's Ronald Agenor, after which he bested Andrei Chesnokov in the semifinals. At last Michael made it to the finals, where his opponent was the No. 3 seed,

All charged up, Michael Chang savors a winning point during a match against John McEnroe at the 1991 U.S. Open.

Stefan Edberg of Sweden. Once again, Michael came from behind and won. Just 17 years old, Michael was the youngest male ever to win a Grand Slam singles title. It was the first French Open victory for an American player since Tony Trabert in 1955.

By calling himself an "evangelist with a racket" in his victory speech, Michael revealed a side of himself that had only been hinted at during matches, when he would often pull a Bible from his workout bag and read from it. "God has an idea for me," he told reporters. "To spread his word through tennis. I realized God gave me talent at this young age. It is what enables me to make contact with the world." Michael, who had been baptized in 1987 when he first started on the pro circuit, was so inspired by reading the Bible that he

Chang falls to his knees in victorious relief after defeating Ivan Lendl of Czechoslovakia at the 1989 French Open.

continued with Bible study classes while on tour. He and his family belong to the Chinese Christian Church of Thousand Oaks, of which Michael's grandfather had been a founding member, and which held a special sermon honoring Michael a few months after his victory.

The week after the French Open, Reebok ran full-page ads in the *New York Times,* the *Los Angeles Times, USA Today,* and the *Boston Globe,* honoring Michael's achievement and that of another 17-year-old Reebok representative, Arantxa Sanchez Vicario, who had won the French women's singles title. The ad copy ran, "Some kids go to Paris to study history. Others go to make it."

Michael's endorsements for Reebok shoes and clothes, Prince rackets, Yale locks, Nissin noodles, Longines watches, and other products were already earning him an income in excess of $1 million a year. His tournament winnings showed signs of reaching that level as well, but he reportedly got an allowance of just $100 a month. Despite money and fame, he was still just a kid, and kind of a shy kid at that. During a guest appearance on "The Tonight Show" in August 1989, Johnny Carson asked him how a recent date with a girlfriend went, especially since he didn't have a driver's license yet. Michael blushed, confessing, "My parents came with us." He eventually got his driver's license in 1991.

After his French Open win, the onus was upon Michael to deliver on his newly acquired promise as the next Great American Tennis Hero. John McEnroe swore he'd drop his tennis shorts if Michael made it to the finals at the next Grand Slam event. Unfortunately, Michael had bad luck and didn't make it past the quarterfinals at Wimbledon, or at the U.S. Open that year.

Chang scores another winning point in his defeat of Francisco Roig of Spain at the 1989 French Open.

13

By the end of 1989 Michael's packed schedule showed 47 wins out of 63 matches, as well as 10 exhibition games. But after his 18th and last ATP event of that year, Michael sustained a stress injury to his hip, which put a damper on his career for awhile. In early December, after playing in the Nabisco Masters, Michael was practicing at the ATP headquarters in Ponte Vedra, Florida. While returning to the middle of the court from a wide backhand, Michael felt a pain in his leg. Dr. Robert Kerlan of the Kerlan/Jobe Orthopedic Clinic in Inglewood, California, diagnosed the injury as an unusual fracture to the hip bone and advised Michael to remain off the pro tour for at least three to six months.

Michael left Kerlan's care after only a month and a half, and rejoined the ATP tour in Memphis at the end of February 1990, but he lost a match in the first round and decided to forego the next two ATP events. He admitted he hadn't given his hip injury enough time to repair. He won a Volvo nontour event in Chicago, but in the following months lost matches at the Japan Open, the German Open, and the Italian Open. His ranking dropped from No. 5 to No. 14. That year, however, he reached the quarterfinals at the French Open and the fourth round at Wimbledon, and helped the U.S. Davis Cup team to victory over Australia. He also reached the quarters of the inaugural Grand Slam Cup tournament, for which he received nearly half a million dollars in prize money.

He played for the Grand Slam Cup again in 1991, winning over Jim Courier, Pat McEnroe, and Ivan Lendl before losing to Davis Wheaton in the final round. Also that year, Michael reached the quarterfinals at the French Open and the fourth round at the U.S. Open, but lost in the opening round at Wimbledon. He consistently reached the quarterfinals in tour events in Brussels, Indian Wells, and Hong Kong, as well as at the U.S. Men's Clay Court Championships.

Michael didn't return to the top 10 until 1992, when he won the Newsweek Champions Cup in March. Seeded No. 5, he made it to the third round of that year's French Open, losing to Nicklas Kulti. He went on to represent the U.S. at the 1992 Olympic Games in Barcelona, but was defeated in the second round. Later that year, he reached the semifinals at the U.S. Open and was runner-up at the 1992 Grand Slam Cup. He won three tour events in 1992, including wins over Jim Courier in San Francisco, Andrei Chesnokov in Indian Wells, and Alberto Mancino in Key Biscayne.

Seeded No. 7, Michael reached the quarterfinal rounds at both the U.S. Open and the Grand Slam Cup in 1993, and he won five singles titles in tour events in Jakarta, Osaka, Cincinnati, Kuala Lumpur, and Beijing. In 1994 Michael remains in the top 10. Seeded No. 8, he made it to the third round of the French Open. He won the U.S. Pro Indoor tournament in Philadelphia, with an upset over Jim Courier in the semifinals and a straight set win over Paul Haarhuis in the final round. He won tour events in Jakarta and Hong Kong, and his victory in Atlanta was his first clay court tournament win since the 1989 French Open. Michael continues to play tennis in Grand Slam and tour events. He owns a home in Henderson, Nevada, and enjoys bass fishing in his spare time.

Sammy Lee, photographed after winning the 1953
James E. Sullivan Memorial Trophy.

Sammy
Lee

DR. SAMMY LEE WAS THE FIRST ASIAN AMERICAN TO win an Olympic gold medal, which he did two Olympic years in a row. Committed to two goals in life—becoming an Olympic diver and an ear doctor—Sammy Lee succeeded in both. Born on August 1, 1920, he was the youngest child and only son of Soonkee and Eunkee Rhee, natives of Seoul, Korea, who immigrated to America after Korea was annexed by the Japanese in 1910. Sammy's mother, Eunkee, was in fact the first Korean woman ever to enter the United States. When Sammy was born, the Rhees were living in the San Joaquin Valley of California, attempting to make a living by farming. Soonkee, who had renounced Buddhism when he left Korea, gave his son a Christian first name, Samuel, and the last name of Lee because so many Americans thought that was what he meant when he said "Rhee."

When Sammy was four years old, the Rhees' farmhouse in the valley was destroyed by fire, and the family relocated to Highland Park, near Los Angeles. Soonkee opened a grocery business, and the family lived above it. Sammy was spoiled, and he had trouble adjusting to the self-disciplinary demands of public school. After he had enrolled at Yorkdale Grammar School, a teacher recommended that he be kept out of school for a year because he was still too immature to obey rules. Soonkee agreed to delay Sammy's entrance for another year, teaching him some self-restraint, as well as elementary reading and writing.

During that year of home schooling, Sammy was exposed to his first Mansei, a traditional play shown to Korean children, illustrating the brutalities committed against Korean students who marched in rebellion against Japanese rule in 1919. Sammy was deeply affected by the depiction of

17

hundreds of Koreans being beheaded by the Japanese. Though Soonkee tried to reason that the play showed the triumph of the Korean spirit, Sammy adopted an anti-Japanese attitude that would influence his actions throughout early adulthood. Even though Soonkee explained that the Japanese in America were Americans, unlike the Japanese who still occupied Korea, Sammy began to hate the Japanese wherever he found them, and once even threatened his neighbors, the Watanabes, with a knife.

At age seven Sammy was finally enrolled in elementary school. He excelled easily because of his father's home tutoring, but he began to experience the cruel discrimination against Asians that made him realize how others perceived him. He had fistfights with boys who mistakenly called him a "Jap" and began to skip school often enough that his father considered sending him to private school. Fortunately, Sammy's second-grade teacher at Yorkdale recognized that he was just bored and gave him more tasks to do in school, such as managing the playground equipment at recess. Sammy began focusing his abundant energy on sports and soon realized that being athletic could lead to popularity in school.

At the onset of the Great Depression in the 1930s, Soonkee lost his business and was forced to move his family into a poor Los Angeles neighborhood, where he opened a restaurant. Sammy, by then an 11-year-old fourth-grader, was small for his age but quickly learned to defend himself in constant street fights with neighborhood kids, a diverse mix of racial minorities. Concerned about his son's welfare, Soonkee moved his restaurant to a better area after two years, returning again to Highland Park.

Sammy reunited with all his old friends, who accepted him warmly because of his prowess in sports. He began swimming at the Brookside Park pool, which was only open to minorities one day a week. Sammy possessed natural physical coordination and loved swimming and diving. One day when Sammy was in the sixth grade, his father took him to downtown Los Angeles to see the flags on display in honor of the Olympic Games. Upon sight of the hundreds of flags from nations the world over, Sammy decided that he would someday be an Olympic champion.

Soon after, at the public pool, he befriended an African American boy named Hart Crum, who taught Sammy the five basic competitive dives—the swan, the backward dive, the gainer, the cutaway, and the combination twist. Over the summer he practiced diving with Hart, and during the academic year he vied for recognition at Burbank Junior High School. His seventh-grade teacher, Walter Koerper, paid Sammy special attention because he admired the "Oriental mind and drive" and wanted to groom Sammy to excel the way a previous Asian student had. When Sammy learned that that student was Japanese, he became determined to do even better. He hated being associated with the Japanese, despite the fact that teachers saw no distinction between Asians of different ethnicities. Sammy saw himself in competition with the Japanese and used his hatred as fuel for his ego. To a large degree, it worked for him. By the eighth grade he was an excellent athlete, the school's cheerleader, and president of his class.

At 17, Sammy entered Benjamin Franklin High School. Older than other kids in his grade but smaller in

stature, he was again determined to make an impact. He made
the junior varsity football team as quarterback and practiced
gymnastics, which helped him in the somersaulting and body-
spiraling required for diving. He entered the junior division
Southern California city diving competition and won. A
Japanese American from Hollywood High School won the
senior title; Sammy could hardly wait to turn 18 so he could
compete against him.

Sammy realized that to be a champion, he needed a
swim coach. Hart had already taught him everything he knew,
but Sammy was doubtful he'd find a coach willing to teach a
Korean. When the Los Angeles Invitational Swim and Diving
meet converged at the L.A. Swim Stadium, Sammy and Hart
went to watch. They were able to practice diving off the
boards between meets because their skin color blended in with
that of the visiting Hawaiian team's.

While diving Sammy caught the attention of Jim
Ryan, the well-known coach of champions. Ryan had an
abrasive, antagonistic style of communication that deeply
upset Sammy, but he endured the abuse because Ryan promised to make him "the greatest diver in the world." Later,
Sammy learned Ryan's true motivation. Ryan had coached
Farid Samaika, the Egyptian who won the Olympic diving
gold medal in 1928, a decision later reversed because, Ryan
believed, the Olympic committee was prejudiced. Ryan vowed
to return to the Olympics someday with another winner. He
pegged Sammy for that spot.

Ryan got his new protégé a summer job as a locker
room attendant at the L.A. Swim Stadium, where one of his
coworkers was a young Esther Williams. After full days of

work Ryan coached Sammy, along with another diver, Dick Smith of the University of Southern California, on the finer points of diving. In the winter Sammy and Dick practiced diving into sand pits dug out of Ryan's backyard. Sammy spent all his free time with Ryan, but still managed to get As in school. When the Southern California diving meets rolled around again, Sammy took the senior title easily.

By his last year of high school Sammy had achieved the notoriety he had set out for. An outstanding athlete, an A student, and popular with teachers and peers alike, he did not hesitate to consider running for president of the student body. The school's vice principal, however, asked him to back down because the student body presidency had never been held by

With lips clenched and body taut, Sammy Lee hits the water during the 1948 Olympic men's high-diving competition. He took the gold medal.

21

a nonwhite. Sammy had already been exposed to his share of bigotry. Undaunted, he ran for student body president and won. When he graduated in 1939, he was chosen as valedictorian of his class and won that year's prestigious Alumni Award.

With all his success, Sammy thought getting a scholarship to college would be no problem. At Ryan's suggestion, he applied to UCLA, declaring to the admissions committee his dual dream of becoming a doctor and an Olympic diver. The UCLA committee, balking at what they perceived to be hubris, awarded the scholarship to someone else. USC offered Sammy only a half-tuition scholarship, so Sammy agreed to attend Occidental College, which offered him full financial assistance.

The summer before college Sammy returned to his job as locker room attendant, but already he was planning to qualify for the Olympic team the following year. He competed in his first national championship in Santa Barbara, placing fourth on both the three-meter board and tower events. Ryan wasn't happy with Sammy's performance, but he was even less happy with that of his other diving student, Dick Smith, who was spending too much time with his girlfriend. Ryan decided to quit coaching Dick and concentrate all his attention on Sammy.

Sportswriters were already starting to notice Sammy as the first Korean American male to reach big-time diving, calling him "The Yellow Peril from the Pacific Coast." Sammy's momentum was broken, however, when Great Britain declared war on Germany and the 1940 Olympics were canceled. Because of the disruption caused by World War II, it would be several years before Sammy would get a shot at the Olympic tryouts.

During the war Ryan took off for Egypt to open a diving school with Samaika, leaving Sammy to train by himself. Sammy continued to dive on the Occidental team, winning them several intercollegiate trophies. Over the summer he worked again at the L.A. Swim Stadium, this time promoted to lifeguard. At season's end he was reunited with Ryan, whose swim school deal had fallen through.

Sammy's second year at college was tougher than his first. His grades fell to Cs and he began to doubt whether he could still pursue diving and take premedical courses. However, when the Japanese attacked Pearl Harbor in 1941, the winter of his junior year, Sammy's old hatred flared up again. He became more determined than ever to beat the Japanese, who had "stolen" the Olympic diving medals from the Americans in 1932. In 1942, in the spring after the attack, Sammy attended his first national indoor meet, sponsored by the Amateur Athletic Union (AAU). He placed only third in the 3-meter event, but he knew he had it in him to be a champion.

During his last year of college, Sammy's premed advisor, Dr. Raymond Selly, jolted him with the news that he would not be recommending him for medical school. Sammy consulted his father, who mysteriously promised him that, when the time came, he would have Selly's recommendation. In the meantime Sammy worked hard at raising his grades. Because of the war there was little public interest in competitive sports, and by not entering national meets, Sammy had more time to study. When Sammy's father died unexpectedly that year, Sammy discovered he had made good on his promise; a few days before his death, he had spoken to Dr. Selly, who agreed to recommend Sammy for medical school. Sammy graduated with nearly straight As in his final semester, silently thanking his father for believing in him.

Accepted at USC's medical school, he enrolled in the army's specialized training program for doctors, automatically making him an army private first class, with fully paid tuition and a much-needed monthly stipend. He occasionally accepted invitations for diving exhibitions, and at one such event, a benefit for the Southern California Chinese Association, he met Roz Wong, the lovely young woman who would eventually become his wife.

Sammy Lee, his wife, Roz, his mother, and his new baby daughter, Pamela, move into their new house in Garden Grove, California, in 1955.

The army program was an intensive two years and nine months, culminating in the M.D. degree. Sammy received nearly failing grades in his first semester. This time, patriotism motivated him to do better. He had completely overcome his bias against Japanese when he witnessed the sufferings of his Japanese American friends from college, who were uprooted to internment camps during the war. Though he debated whether going to war as a soldier might be better, he was assured that becoming a doctor would in fact be one of the greatest efforts he could make for his country. With the help of a close-knit study group, he succeeded in bringing up his grades. He graduated from medical school in June 1946.

Promoted to first lieutenant, Sammy continued his education under the army program, even though the war was over. He was assigned to Orange County Hospital for his internship. Despite his heavy new responsibilities, he still found time for diving. That fall, he placed first in the 10-meter tower event at the AAU championship. The 1948 Olympics were only two years away.

Sammy fulfilled the rest of his army obligation at McCornack Army Hospital in Pasadena, training at the Pasadena Athletic Club and the L.A. Swim Stadium. He was assigned to anesthesiology at first, but moved to the ear, nose, and throat section; ever since a childhood ear infection had been "miraculously" cured by a specialist, he had wanted to be an ear doctor. In June of 1948, a month before the Olympic tryouts in Detroit, Sammy was relieved of all hospital duties so he could train.

He easily made the Olympic team that year, along with Bruce Harlan and Miller Anderson, scoring the highest point average ever recorded on the 10-meter tryouts. In

London, where the 1948 Olympics were held, the U.S. team triumphed in both diving events. In the three-meter spring-board event, Harlan took the gold medal, Miller the silver, and Sammy the bronze. For the tower event, Miller was taken out by an injury during practice, so Harlan took the silver, and Mexico's Capilla the bronze. But Sammy won the gold with his three-and-a-half-turn forward somersault, a dive previously believed to be impossible. He was the first Asian American ever to win an Olympic gold medal.

Afterward the U.S. swim team went on a whirlwind exhibition tour of European army stations, receiving much praise and adulation in Amsterdam, Berlin, and Paris. The French called Sammy "The Coca-Cola Kid" after his dive consisting of a two-and-a-half-turn somersault, open to swan, then somersault again, "the pause that refreshes." Returning from his glory trip to finish his stint at McCornack Hospital, he remained in the army for his residency, becoming a captain at Letterman Army Hospital in San Francisco. The residency lasted three years, interrupted a few times by exhibition diving invitations in New Zealand and Hawaii. Sammy also got engaged to Roz Wong, who was working as a bookkeeper at Letterman. The wedding was almost postponed when the Korean War broke out, but Sammy was spared from service abroad because he could be mistaken for the enemy and, unable to speak Korean, would have no way of talking himself out of trouble. Sammy and Roz were married on October 1, 1950.

Sammy participated in the first Pan American games, but, out of practice, did not perform well. Unwilling to retire a defeated champion, he decided to have a go at the 1952 Olympics and was granted leave from his residency to train, which he estimated could take up to nine months. He was transferred to Fort MacArthur in San Pedro so he could still work as a medical officer while utilizing nearby diving facilities. He came in fourth in the three-meter dive tryouts in Astoria, Long Island, but made the team by placing first in the tower event. He went on to Helsinki, Finland, where the 1952 Olympics were held. This time joined by his wife, Sammy lodged in the Olympic Village with the other athletes. It was his birthday when he claimed Olympic victory in the 10-meter tower event—at 32 the oldest man ever to win that event, and the first to do so two Olympic years in a row.

After the obligatory exhibition tour of army bases in Europe, Sammy returned home and was promoted to major. In August of 1953 he was sent to serve in Seoul, Korea. His mother joked that he should have "U.S. Olympic Champion" tattooed on his chest. While in Korea, he met his uncle on his mother's side for the first time and was reunited with Syngman Rhee, an old friend of his father's and now president of South Korea, who welcomed Sammy warmly, arranging a diving exhibition attended by Korean dignitaries.

In 1953 Sammy was nominated for the James E. Sullivan Award given by the AAU and accepted the award in New York, in a ceremony attended by his mother. Afterward they attended a broadcast of "The Ed Sullivan Show." When Sullivan introduced them to the rest of the studio audience, Sammy's mother stood up and thanked him, much to everyone's amusement, for giving her son his award.

Shortly afterward, Sammy was asked to become the U.S. sports ambassador to Southeast Asia. His three-month tour of duty entailed diving exhibitions, coaching sessions for local divers, press conferences, and publicizing the greatness

Lee in the training pool at Wembley Stadium, England, in 1948.

of America. His itinerary included stops in Japan, Sri Lanka, India, Pakistan, Burma, Vietnam, Turkey, Indonesia, Singapore, Hong Kong, and the Philippines. Much impressed by all he had seen in his travels, he returned to Korea in November of 1954 to find that he had completed his military obligation there and could return home to California.

In 1955 he was invited to speak at President Eisenhower's First White House Conference on Juvenile Delinquency and Physical Fitness. Later that year, on September 5, Sammy and Roz had their first child, Pamela. They later had a son, Sammy junior, born on March 18, 1960. In October 1955 Sammy was released from the army, and the Lees moved to a new home in Orange County. Sammy flourished in private practice, helped by the publicity of his speaking engagements. In 1956 he served as President Eisenhower's personal representative, along with Jesse Owens and Bob Mathias, at the Olympics in Melbourne, Australia. He coached the U.S. women's diving team at the 1960 games in Rome and judged diving events at the next two Olympic Games, in Tokyo (1964) and Mexico City (1968). In 1970 he served on President Nixon's Council on Physical Fitness and Sports, and two years later was again one of the President's personal representatives to the Olympics, in Munich, this time appointed chairman.

Meanwhile, Sammy was cultivating a rewarding second career as a diving coach. Once, after he had spoken at a high school in Santa Ana, a young diver named Bob Webster approached Sammy for coaching. Sammy took him on and helped Webster win gold medals in the 1960 and 1964 Olympics. Later Sammy took another diver under his wing, a young man named Greg Louganis, who went on to win a silver medal in the Olympics of 1976 and the gold in both diving events at the 1984 games. Kitty O'Neil, a young woman who had been deaf since childhood, was another of Sammy's students. Although she never made it to the Olympics as a diver, she became one of the country's best female stock car drivers. When *Silent Victory*, a movie about O'Neil's life, was made for television, Sammy was asked to play himself, opposite Stockard Channing as Kitty.

Overall, Sammy has led an illustrious post-Olympic life. He was given an honorary doctorate degree by Occidental College for his athletic and humanitarian contributions, and in 1984 he was named an outstanding alumnus of the USC School of Medicine. That same year he carried the Olympic Torch part of the way through Koreatown on the day before the games were held in Los Angeles, and was one of the Olympic flag bearers during the opening ceremonies. At the 10th Asian Games, a prelude to the 1988 Olympics in Seoul, he was an honored guest of the Korean Swimming and Diving Federation. In 1986 he was selected as a commissioner for President Reagan's White House Fellows. In 1987 Sammy toured the United States with Olympic swimmer Tracy Caulkins to promote understanding of the James E. Sullivan Award, now considered the most prestigious athletic award not limited to one sport. But in true honor of all of Sammy's achievements, there is also the Sammy Lee Diving Award, voted on by the World Diving Coaches Association and given by the Kalos Kathagos Foundation. Literally, and fittingly, "Kalos Kathogos" means "physical distinction, nobility of mind."

Zubin Mehta, 1979.

ZUBIN MEHTA IS ONE OF THE WORLD'S FOREMOST CON-ductors of classical music. Hailed as "the next Toscanini," he gained adulation from the music community at a young age and has held the world's attention ever since. Throughout his career, his busy schedule has kept pace with his exuberant personality. Since the early 1960s he has maintained music directorships with four world-class orchestras, and has had numerous stints as a guest conductor with symphonies all over the world.

Zubin Mehta was born in Bombay, India, on April 29, 1936, the same day that Arturo Toscanini retired as music director of the New York Philharmonic. Zubin's family are Parsis, descendants of the Zoroastrian sect that fled religious persecution in Persia during the eighth and ninth centuries and settled in Bombay, where they were forbidden to own land but were able to flourish in trade. Zubin's father, Mehli Mehta, neglected his family's textile business and expended his effort on Western music, teaching himself to play the violin. In the 1930s Mehli founded the Bombay String Quartet and the Bombay Symphony, which both proved influential in exposing India to Western music.

Zubin was born into his father's world of classical music, and it seemed inevitable that it would become his lifelong occupation. Mehli began teaching his son the violin and piano when Zubin was seven. Two years later, Mehli left Bombay to study violin with Ivan Galamian in New York. For the four years his father was absent, Zubin continued to study music out of loneliness. By his early teen years Zubin was leading sectional rehearsals of the Bombay Symphony, and by age 16, he had actually conducted a full orchestra rehearsal for the first time.

His parents, however, actually wanted Zubin to become a doctor. His mother, Tehmina, thought medicine would be a more respectable profession. After graduating from St. Mary's, a Jesuit private school, in 1951, Zubin enrolled at St. Xavier's College. He took premedical courses for two years, until one day in zoology class he was confronted with the prospect of dissecting a lizard. Zubin promptly quit school, deciding on a career in music by default.

At age 18, he was off to Vienna, Austria, to attend the state-run Academy of Music. He refined his conducting skills under Hans Swarowsky and also studied piano, the double bass, and musical composition. At the academy Zubin met his first girlfriend, a Canadian voice student named Carmen Lasky. He married her in 1958, a year after he graduated with a degree in conducting.

That same year he won first place in the Liverpool International Conductor's Competition, which entailed a one-year contract as associate conductor of the Royal Liverpool Philharmonic, which he led to critical acclaim in 14 concerts. He also conducted in Belgium and Yugoslavia for the Jeunesses Musicales, an exchange program for young musicians, and took second place at the Tanglewood competition in Massachusetts.

Throughout 1960 and 1961 Zubin was invited to serve as guest conductor for major orchestras around the world, beginning with the Vienna Symphony Orchestra. Then, as famed maestros from Berlin to Philadelphia to Prague seemed to fall ill one after the other, Zubin was asked to step in as a substitute. Reflecting back on the early stages of his career, Zubin once told a reporter, "I sometimes think my success was due almost entirely to the misfortunes of my elderly colleagues."

On July 26, 1960, Zubin made his New York Philharmonic debut at an outdoor concert at Lewissohn Stadium. Later that year, he conducted the Israel Philharmonic in Tel Aviv for the first time. When the conductor of the Montreal Symphony Orchestra, Igor Markevitch, resigned due to failing health, Zubin became his substitute for two weeks in 1960. In January of 1961, the Montreal Symphony appointed Zubin its music director.

*Zubin Mehta leads the
New York Philharmonic
as the pianist Vladimir
Horowitz returns to the
concert stage after a
25 year absence.*

Before the year was out Zubin would find himself with a second appointment. In 1961 Zubin conducted a concert with the Los Angeles Philharmonic and was asked back for more, after which the orchestra's music director, Georg Solti, abruptly resigned, angry that the board of director's had not consulted him first. By November Zubin was asked to take his place. The following year, when his first concert season with the Los Angeles Philharmonic began, Zubin, at age 26, was the orchestra's youngest-ever music director. Since he had not relinquished his post in Montreal, he was also the first man to hold that position for two North American symphony orchestras concurrently.

Dividing his attentions between two major orchestras in distant cities took its toll on Zubin's personal life. In 1962 Zubin relocated to Los Angeles, leaving behind his wife, Carmen, and their two children, Zarina and Merwan. Fortunately Zubin's brother, Zarin, lived in Montreal, and he promised to look after Zubin's family. Zarin, an accountant, took such good care of them, in fact, that after Zubin divorced Carmen, Zarin married her. Zarin and Carmen eventually had children of their own.

Zubin's musical life, however, went much more smoothly. In 1962 he took the Montreal Symphony Orchestra on tour for the first time. They played eight concerts in Russia, two in Paris, and another in Vienna. In the former Soviet republic, Zubin showed his disapproval of police states by goose-stepping offstage and crying "Revolt!" to visitors backstage. In Vienna, the capital of Western classical music, the symphony received a 20-minute standing ovation, 14 curtain calls, and two encores. In a short time, Zubin had transformed the Montreal Symphony into an orchestra of international quality. He served as its music director until 1967.

Zubin's achievement with the Los Angeles Philharmonic was no less dramatic. When Zubin took the baton, the orchestra had only made one tour since its founding in 1919. During Zubin's 16-year tenure, the symphony toured 14 times. Through Zubin's leadership, the list of the top five American orchestras—in New York, Philadelphia, Boston, Cleveland, and Chicago—became known as the "top six," now including Los Angeles. In 1967 Zubin took the Los Angeles Philharmonic to Carnegie Hall for its New York debut. He then combined the Montreal and Los Angeles orchestras at Expo '67 for a performance of Berlioz's *Symphonie Fantastique.* In May of that year Zubin stepped down from the Montreal directorship, and by the fall he was touring with the Los Angeles symphony for two months straight, including stops in Athens, Paris, Vienna, and his hometown of Bombay.

Zubin pledged allegiance to another country as well, the home of the Israel Philharmonic Orchestra, with which he had first appeared in 1961 and gone on tour in 1966. He had come to love the country through its symphony. When the six-day Arab-Israeli war of 1967 broke out, Zubin dropped everything and rushed to Tel Aviv before the airport closed down so he could conduct a series of concerts with the Israel Philharmonic Orchestra. Later that year, he was named the IPO's musical adviser and, two years after that, music director.

He conducted for soldiers during the Yom Kippur war, with Isaac Stern, Daniel Barenboim, and Pinchas Zuckerman playing as soloists. In 1971 Zubin took the IPO to Germany for the Berlin Festival. The orchestra had never played there before. After its performance of Mahler's First, the German audience responded with an extended ovation. Zubin ended the concert with Israel's national anthem. The audience didn't recognize the music, but when they saw the musicians standing, tears running down their faces, they gradually rose to their feet.

Zubin was honored in a speech by then-president of Israel Ephraim Katzir, and just before Golda Meir passed away in 1978, she said, "It's heartwarming to see a man like Zubin Mehta become so attached to Israel. He has never failed us. Whenever there is a war and the country is in danger, he appears, regardless of his other commitments. For us it's an extremely emotional experience."

To help fund the IPO's international tours, Zubin cofounded the American Friends of the IPO with Philadelphia financier Frederic R. Mann. Itzhak Perlman serves as cochair of the AFIPO along with Zubin. In 1983 Zubin's tenure as the orchestra's music director was extended for life. He has also received honorary degrees from the Hebrew University of Jerusalem, Tel Aviv University, and the Weizman Institute.

Until 1978 Zubin was still enjoying his time in Los Angeles. The city afforded him the opportunity to dabble in experimental contemporary music, which included appearances with Frank Zappa and the Mothers of Invention. Zubin also socialized with Hollywood celebrities, which earned him a reputation of being something of a playboy. In 1969 he married the actress Nancy Kovak, and a few years later they purchased Steve McQueen's palatial home in Brentwood for nearly half a million dollars.

In 1978 Zubin ended his contract with the Los Angeles Philharmonic and accepted the challenge of New York. He had been in the running to direct the New York Philharmonic once before, in 1967, with Leonard Bernstein's scheduled retirement just two years away. But Zubin had expressed no interest in the position at the time, explaining to the press rather flippantly that "Artistically, it would not be a step up for me." The New York Philharmonic subsequently canceled Zubin's scheduled appearances with them and hired Pierre Boulez as music director in 1971. Boulez resigned after six years, and by then Zubin seemed to have changed his opinion about New York. "It's the absolute center of the performing arts," he said in an interview. "Competition can only breed excellence."

Despite a generally lukewarm reception from jaded New York critics, who tend to be blasé about their hometown orchestra in the face of constant exposure to world-class visiting programs, Zubin managed to sustain public interest

Mehta in a pensive mood as he conducts the Israel Philharmonic Orchestra.

in the New York Philharmonic. He averaged an attendance rate of more than 90% for his concerts at Avery Fisher Hall and raised subscription levels to a record high of 33,000. He toured with the orchestra in the former Soviet Union and throughout Europe. In 1984 he led the New York Philharmonic on an Asian tour of 13 cities, including New Delhi, Calcutta, and Bombay.

The concerts in India were met with much fanfare, including billboards announcing his arrival and widespread exposure on national television in the country's first live telecast of Western music. Despite his many years in California and New York, Zubin still thinks of himself as an Indian. "Those roots you just can't take away," he told a reporter. He can still speak his Indian dialect, loves Indian food, and abstains from alcohol, coffee, and cigarettes in obeyance to the Zoroastrian religion. At the conclusion of his visit to Bombay, he conducted the "Stars and Stripes Forever" wearing a Dugli, the Parsi ceremonial dress. When asked by an Indian reporter where Zubin considered his home, he replied,

Vocal soloists Kathleen Battle and Maureen Forrester flank the podium as Zubin Mehta leads the New York Philharmonic in its 10,000th performance.

"I have homes in many cities—Los Angeles, New York, and I feel at home in Vienna, where I studied, and in Israel. But there is no place where I have the feeling of warmth as here in Bombay, the city where I was born."

Zubin's whole family now lives in Southern California. Zubin still owns his Brentwood home with his wife, and he had a townhouse in New York until he resigned from the New York Philharmonic. On November 2, 1988, he announced his departure, scheduled for the end of the 1990–91 season. After 13 years, he had held the position of music director longer than any other conductor in the symphony's history. He refused offers for other music directorships, explaining in a statement, "I must at this juncture pursue other artistic endeavors which have to do with less administrative activity than that with which a music director is usually involved."

Those "other artistic endeavors" include opera, which has been an important facet of Zubin's musical life since 1965, when he made his Metropolitan Opera debut conducting Giuseppe Verdi's *Aïda* in New York. His subsequent performances at the Met included *Carmen, Tosca, Turandot,* and the 1967 world premiere of Marvin Levy's *Mourning Becomes Electra.* Over the years, he has conducted *Tristan und Isolde* in Berlin, Vienna, Rome, London, Montreal, and Los Angeles. He has also led orchestras performing *Otello, Don Giovanni,* and *Samson et Delila.* After his retirement from the New York Philharmonic in 1991, he conducted several European operatic productions, including those at the Bastille Opera in Paris and the Royal Opera in London. Every spring, Zubin still conducts opera in Florence, at the Maggio Musicale, of which he is an artistic adviser.

Wayne Wang at the time of the filming
of Chan Is Missing.

Wayne Wang

FILMMAKER WAYNE WANG IS BEST KNOWN FOR DIRECTing the critically acclaimed hit movie, *The Joy Luck Club,* based on Amy Tan's best-selling novel of the same name. Though his earlier independent features dealing with Chinese American themes were all well received, the success of *The Joy Luck Club* has proven that such themes can have universal appeal to mainstream audiences.

Wayne Wang was born in January 1949, 12 days after the Communist revolution in China, and 6 days after his parents fled to Hong Kong. Wayne's father came from a merchant family, and as a child he had worked with the U.S. Navy in the port of Tsingtao. He developed an affinity for American movies and named his second son after John Wayne. In Hong Kong, Wayne's father ran an export-import business, selling everything from seaweed to sheet iron. He transferred his love of American movies to Wayne, raising him on a steady diet of B movies and Audie Murphy films.

Wayne attended Catholic and Jesuit schools, which were taught in both Cantonese and English. He spoke Mandarin at home, but his parents were very pro-American, imbuing him with an almost mythical sense of the country by telling him things like, "In America, the oranges are bigger." It seemed inevitable that Wayne would eventually come to America himself, especially after China's Cultural Revolution began causing turbulence in Hong Kong. In 1967, at age 18, Wayne left for the United States on a student visa.

College was a period of awkward assimilation for Wayne. At Foothill College in California, he tried to immerse himself in the typical student life of drinking, drugs, and political demonstrations. He switched majors from commercial art to painting and ended his formal education in 1973 with a master's degree in film and television from the California College of Arts and Crafts. But because breaking into Hollywood would have taken at least five years of struggle after graduating, Wayne returned to Hong Kong and got a head start in the industry there.

He encountered many problems on his first job as assistant director of the Chinese segments in the 1974 film *Golden Needles.* He went on to become director of a popular Hong Kong television series, "Below the Lion Rock," but the comedic soap opera genre conflicted with his higher ideals about filmmaking. After three months he returned to California with his first wife, Terrel Seltzer, whom he had just married.

Living in San Francisco, he became immersed in community activism on behalf of immigrants in Chinatown. His experience training Chinese immigrants for jobs inspired *Chan Is Missing,* Wayne's first film and the first feature ever made using an all-Asian-American cast. A detective story spliced with slices of Chinese immigrant life, *Chan Is Missing* used nonprofessional actors and was shot on 16mm black-and-white film at a total cost of only $22,000. Released in 1982 by New Yorker Films, the independent feature garnered little attention until its run at the Museum of Modern Art as part of the 1982 Filmex and the New Directors/New Films series. For a small film, *Chan* made a big splash, eventually grossing more than $1 million, about 50 times its production cost.

After the success of his first film, Wayne, by this time an American citizen, flirted with the idea of crossing over immediately to Hollywood. He pitched stories to major studios, worked on several scripts, and almost signed on to do

a movie with Ron Howard's production company. But Wayne decided to stick to his ideals. He and his wife Terrel had already been working on a script called *Dim Sum: A Little Bit of Heart,* and Wayne decided to make that his next independent feature. In the summer of 1983 he went ahead and shot enough footage for nearly half the movie, which originally centered around five Chinese American women. After about six months of filming, Wayne realized that the complexity of the story was becoming problematic, so he halted production, reworked the script, and resumed shooting in June 1984.

During the making of *Dim Sum,* Wayne also decided that his marriage wasn't working, so he divorced Terrel and married Cora Miao, a popular Hong Kong actress whom he had cast as a supporting actress in the film. The final version of *Dim Sum* focuses on just three main characters, depicting

Director Wayne Wang prepares to shoot a scene from **The Joy Luck Club**.

the cultural and generational tensions between a Chinese widow, her American-born daughter, and an uncle. The film, financed mostly by San Francisco architect and real estate developer Vincent Tai, was finished at a final cost of $500,000, about twice the original budget. *Dim Sum* opened at Cannes in 1985 to much praise from the critics.

With *Chan Is Missing* as a sort of introduction to the Chinese American community, and *Dim Sum* as a specific story set within that context, Wayne resolved much of his own inner conflict about being Chinese American. He now felt ready to make a move toward more mainstream Hollywood directing. He received an assignment to direct *Slamdance,* based on a screenplay by Don Opper about a cartoonist who becomes implicated in a series of crimes set in L.A.'s underground nightclub and art scene. With a budget of $4.5 million, Wayne directed *Slamdance* on a tight shooting schedule starting on August 13, 1986, and finishing on October 6. The film stars Tom Hulce and Mary Elizabeth Mastrantonio, and features character actor Harry Dean Stanton, as well as the musicians Adam Ant and John Doe. Though received warmly at the 1987 Cannes Film Festival, *Slamdance* didn't do as well in movie theaters and passed quickly onto the shelves of video rental stores.

Wayne's next project was *Eat a Bowl of Tea,* based on the 1961 Louis Chu novel set in New York's Chinatown of the late 1940s, when the War Brides Act finally permitted Chinese American servicemen to bring over their Chinese wives, who had been barred from entering the U.S. prior to World War II. In the lead roles of the film's newlyweds, Wayne cast his second wife, Cora, and handsome Chinese

American actor Russell Wong. Backed by Columbia Pictures with a budget under $2 million, *Eat a Bowl of Tea* was shot in Hong Kong using period sets recreating postwar New York Chinatown. Filming in Hong Kong was a unique experience. The budget included line items providing money for such things as paying off the triads, Hong Kong's crime gangs, and "the offer of the pigs," without which the local film crew wouldn't work.

 Eat a Bowl of Tea was released in 1989 in New York, San Francisco, and Los Angeles, and by then Wayne had already shot portions of his next project, *Life Is Cheap . . . but Toilet Paper is Expensive,* using some of the same cast and crew members in Hong Kong. Another independent, Hong Kong–financed picture, *Life Is Cheap* is an offbeat black comedy about a Chinese Japanese American entangled with Hong Kong's seedy underworld. The film again features Cora Miao and blends documentary-style footage with fictional elements based on factual material. The Motion Picture Association of America gave the movie an X rating, but Wayne refused to accept it, insisting that the violence and seaminess of his film was clearly distinguishable from obscene pornography. *Life Is Cheap* opened in New York in August 1990 with an unprecedented rating of A for Adult.

 It seemed that Wayne was back to doing films about Chinese Americans at the expense of becoming a big Hollywood director. But when he accepted his next project, he got the opportunity to do both. In 1989 Wayne had met with writer Amy Tan to discuss the possibility of turning her best-selling novel about four Chinese women and their American-born daughters into a movie. Tan had already received at least five offers from other people who wanted to make the film version of *The Joy Luck Club*, but until she met Wayne, she wasn't even convinced that the book should be a movie.

After their conversation swapping personal histories over tea at the Clift Hotel in San Francisco, Tan knew Wayne was the right choice for director. Wayne, like Tan, was hesitant at first but inevitably drawn to the project. "I didn't want to do another Chinese movie," he later said in a newspaper interview. "Yet I loved the book . . . . I felt the book transcended just being Chinese."

A few months later, Oscar-winning screenwriter Ron Bass (*Rain Man, Sleeping With the Enemy*) agreed to cowrite the script with Tan. Bass helped streamline the book's sprawling mosaic of 16 interwoven stories by implementing voice-overs and creating the farewell party scene that recurs throughout the film, serving as the "wraparound" device that anchors the

On the set of **The Joy Luck Club,** *from left to right, Lisa Lu, Tsai Chin, Wayne Wang, and France Nuyen.*

plot lines to a linear context. With Bass's help, Wayne and Tan realized that *Joy Luck* could be made into a mainstream, commercial movie without sacrificing its rich thematic content.

Joy Luck's executive producers, Janet Yang and Oliver Stone, helped circulate the final script. Expecting that its all-Asian and mostly female cast would put off most major studios, they were pleasantly surprised when Walt Disney Studios agreed to finance the picture with a $10.6 million budget, which was low for a major studio film, but still much higher than Wayne had ever worked with.

Five months before production, which was slated for the fall of 1992, Wayne began the formidable task of casting the film's numerous characters, which included a total of 60 speaking parts, with 50 calling for women. He stuck to two general principles—Asian roles would be played by Asians, not Caucasians made up to look Asian, but specifically Chinese roles would not be restricted to Chinese actors. Because of the dearth of good roles for Asians in film, Wayne felt committed to providing opportunities to actors of all Asian backgrounds, as long as they were right for the roles.

Some of the parts required actresses to speak Mandarin, so open casting calls were held in Los Angeles, San Francisco, and New York. Hundreds of real-life mothers and daughters showed up to audition together. They had all related strongly to Tan's book. At one open call, Wayne observed, "I felt there were at least 400 Joy Luck Club stories in that room." Wayne decided to use professional actresses for the eight leading characters. But he also had to find actresses who could play them at different ages, because of the movie's many flashback scenes. "It was like a puzzle," Wayne

*Wayne Wang
on the set of*
Chan Is Missing.

told a reporter. "Right from the start, I knew that if we cast this movie right, my job would be half done. And if we didn't, I would be in a lot of trouble."

For Wayne, the casting and preparation of a movie, along with editing, are the most enjoyable parts of filmmaking. He believes that the actual shooting on the set is "only 10% of the process . . . often nothing more than perfunctory execution." *The Joy Luck Club* took 10 weeks of filming in San Francisco, and another 4 on location in China. After a few problems while shooting overseas, such as constant rain and being chased away from a remote Chinese village, Wayne decided to finish the China scenes by building period sets within an abandoned chocolate factory in San Francisco.

But the movie finished on time and under budget. After an L.A. opening hosted by actress and *Joy Luck* fan Annette Bening, the movie opened nationally in September and October of 1993 and went on to gross more than $32 million in the United States alone. Widely perceived as a "breakthrough" hit, Wayne characterizes *Joy Luck* as "the first so-called Chinese American film that's accessible and very universal." He hopes that his success will give other Asian American directors such as Ang Lee, Peter Wang, and Tony Chan more opportunities to do bigger-budget films, too, and perhaps Wayne will even be able to produce them.

Immediately after *Joy Luck* opened, Wayne began working with Tan and Bass on the script for Tan's second novel, *The Kitchen God's Wife.* But first he wants to "step away from the Chinese thing for a while." He has recently finished directing *Smoke,* which is based on an op-ed piece written by novelist Paul Auster for the *New York Times.* Wayne describes the project as "a strange Christmas story" about a Brooklyn smoke shop owner and the intertwining lives of the shop's customers. For Wayne, whose influences range from Frank Capra to Yasujiro Ozu to Martin Scorsese, the most important element of any projects he takes on is that they are "just good, strong, human stories."

*Kristi Yamaguchi wins the Ladies Single Skating competition at the
1992 U.S. National Figure Skating Championship in Orlando, Florida.*

KRISTI TSUYA YAMAGUCHI WAS BORN ON JULY 12, 1971, in Hayward, California, in the San Francisco Bay Area, and raised in nearby Fremont. Her parents, Carole Doi, a medical secretary, and Jim Yamaguchi, a dentist, met at the University of California at Berkeley, married, and had three children: Kristi, her older sister, Lori, and her younger brother, Brett. Kristi was born with clubfeet, a deformity of the foot easily treated by corrective shoes and, in Kristi's case, leaving no long-term damage.

When Kristi was five years old, she saw Dorothy Hamill win the 1976 Olympic gold medal for women's singles skating and began imagining herself in the Winter Games. Seeing professional ice-skating shows further nourished her skating fever, and she began taking lessons, demonstrating plenty of natural ability. She was participating in competitions by the time she was eight years of age. When she was nine, she accelerated her training to a rigorous program that involved getting up before dawn and practicing for hours at the local skating rink before going off to elementary school.

Around that time in her career, Kristi met her current singles coach, Christy Kjarsgaard-Ness. They maintained a close working relationship over the years, even though skaters usually change coaches often. In 1983 Kristi found a skating partner, Rudi Galindo, and with the expert instruction of their pairs coach, Jim Hulick, Kristi and Rudi placed fifth in the 1985 National Junior Championships. They improved well enough after that to win first place in 1986. That same year, Kristi began to show prowess in singles events by becoming the Central Pacific junior champion and qualifying to compete for the national junior medal, placing fourth in the event.

Kristi
Yamaguchi

In 1988 she won gold medals for both the singles and pairs categories at the World Junior Championships, which led to her selection by the Women's Sports Foundation as Up-and-Coming Artistic Athlete of the Year. She officially "arrived" in 1989 by winning her first senior title, a gold medal in the pairs division at the National Championships, which took place in Baltimore, Maryland. She also came in second in the singles competition, winning her a total of two medals at the "nationals," which hadn't been done by a female skater since Margaret Graham in 1954.

Kristi's establishment in the annals of women's skating came not without sacrifice. Aside from the years of relentless training, Kristi missed out on living the relatively carefree life of a regular kid. Instead of attending high school with other children her age, she took independent study because she knew it would benefit her career. After the first two years, she decided she needed to have exposure to other kids, so she returned to the grind of early to rise and early to bed, fitting in training, school, then training again. She explained her motivation to *Seventeen* magazine: "Sometimes I just wanted to let loose and not worry about training, but long-term I was aware of what was important to me in life, and that kept me in line."

Kristi's hard work paid off. She went on to compete in the 1989 World Championships, held in Paris, emerging as the sixth-best female singles skater in the world and placing fifth with Rudi in the pairs category. Though it appeared she was well on her way to the Olympics, which was just three years away, Kristi was circumspect. "There are always new skaters coming up," she said in *People* magazine. "Anything could happen."

And a few things did happen that might have derailed anyone less talented. Kristi's singles coach, Kjarsgaard-Ness, got married and moved to Edmonton, in Alberta, Canada. The day after her high school graduation, Kristi also moved to Edmonton to be able to continue skating under the direction of Kjarsgaard-Ness. Rudi decided to move, too, so he could keep on training with Kristi, and the pair shuttled back and forth between Canada and California to train with their pairs coach, Hulick. Within months Kristi suffered the losses of two people who had been big influences—her coach, Hulick, who died of colon cancer in December 1989, and her grandfather on her mother's side, who died at about the same time.

Kristi and Rudi had trouble finding another pairs coach, and at the 1990 World Championships they failed to improve on their fifth-place standing from the previous year. In the singles category, Kristi was able to move up two notches to fourth place. So in May of 1990 Kristi decided to focus solely on singles competition and withdraw completely from the pairs category. It was a difficult decision. "To improve in one or the other," she told a *New York Times* reporter, "I had to choose."

At the same time, Kristi's work was made a bit easier by the July 1990 ruling to eliminate thereafter the compulsory figures from major skating competitions. "Compulsories" or "school figures" are exercises requiring skaters to trace patterns with each foot on the ice, which the judges then examine closely to arrive at a score. The compulsories had always been Kristi's weakest event, but now she could concentrate on the artistic and technical sides of her performance. Her streamlined training regimen improved her standing as a singles skater. By the end of 1990 Kristi was considered one of the

Kristi performs her Original Program at the 1992 U.S.
National Figure Skating Championship.

top three or four female singles skaters worldwide, having won first place in three competitions in a row, including the 1990 Goodwill Games, the Skate America contest in October, and the Nations Cup match in November.

Kristi suffered a minor setback in February 1991 when she lost first place at the National Championships to Tonya Harding of Portland, Oregon. Harding, like Japan's Midori Ito, the 1990 world champion, could land the notoriously difficult triple axel jump. Ito and Harding were the only two women in the world to be able to do so in competition. But Kristi hardly had time to dwell on her failure to place first. The 1991 World Championships were scheduled just a month away in Munich. There, she skated almost perfectly to a gold medal victory.

She also won the world crown at the 1992 World Championships. In her long program, she solidly executed the triple Salchow, another challenging figure-skating move, which had given her trouble in previous competitions. By the time the 1992 Winter Olympics in Albertville, France, rolled around, she held the top titles for female figure skating both nationally and in the world. And yet she still had been unable to execute the triple axel jump. To combat excessive media focus on Kristi's inability to perform that difficult maneuver, Kjarsgaard-Ness insisted to the press that Kristi's triple lutz jump into a triple toe loop combination was equal in difficulty to the triple axel. To erase any doubts about her technical capability—her artistic ability was never a question—Kristi planned seven triples for her skating program.

Kristi needn't have worried. She was the only skater among her competitors to be able to maintain her grace under the Olympic pressure, performing, as one journalist put it, "as if all that mattered was making people smile." Even though Kristi was the reigning world champion, almost everyone expected Midori Ito to win the gold medal and Kristi to take the silver. The press characterized Kristi as the underdog, and this frame of mind took some of the pressure off; if she didn't win the gold in '92, she would have another shot in '94.

So Kristi was free to have fun at the games. While her competitors were off training in other countries, Kristi arrived in Albertville more than a week before her figure-skating competitions would begin so she could march in the opening ceremonies. She also bunked in the Olympic Village and went out dancing with other Olympic athletes. When the time came to focus on the competition, she concentrated on enjoying herself, not just winning, out on the ice.

Skating to the "Blue Danube Waltz" and "Malaguena," Kristi seemed to float through her required and free-skate programs, making far fewer mistakes than her competitors, who all seemed to buckle under the pressure. Kristi, of course, won the gold (Ito took the silver and Nancy Kerrigan the bronze). Though relieved to have whatever pressure she had felt finally taken off, her triumph was in a sense anticlimactic. As she later told *Sports Illustrated*, "I knew I'd done well, and I was happy for that. But I remember thinking, Is that it? This is the Olympics. You've always dreamed of it, always, your whole life. I didn't want it to be over yet." In a profile of Kristi in *Seventeen* magazine, she related the most exciting moment for her at the games. It was just before she went up to the podium to accept her gold medal. She and the other American medal-winner, Kerrigan, were elated. "We were backstage saying, 'Oh my gosh, can you believe this is happening? This is the Olympics!'"

Kristi's down-to-earth attitude also helped her through the post-Olympic media controversy over whether she would receive fewer offers from companies to endorse their products because of the strong anti-Japanese sentiment in the United States at the time. Both sides of Kristi's family had planted their roots in America generations before, though her grandparents had been incarcerated in internment camps, like most other Japanese Americans during World War II. After Kristi's Olympic victory, the business media speculated that more endorsements would be offered to Kerrigan because her image was more in keeping with the public's definition of "all-American." The prejudgments didn't bother Kristi much. After all, she didn't become an ice skater for financial gain.

It is not all fun. During a strenuous workout, Kristi gets some advice from her coach, Christy Kjarsgaard-Ness, prior to competing in the 1992 Winter Olympic Games at Albertville, France.

At the 1992 Winter Olympic Games in Albertville, France, gold medalist Kristi Yamaguchi is flanked by silver medalist Midori Ito and bronze medalist Nancy Kerrigan.

In the end, she received her fair share of commercial exposure. She was featured in fashion magazines such as *Elle, Seventeen,* and *Vogue.* She signed a contract with Kellogg to endorse its Special K cereal, became the spokesperson for DuraSoft Colors contact lenses, and represented the Hoechst Celanese Corporation, a fabric manufacturer, for their "Celebrate Acetate!" fashion campaign. She also got the star treatment that accompanied her status as world-famous celebrity. As part of the U.S. presidential delegation to the 1992 Summer Olympics, headed by Arnold Schwarzenegger, she flew to Barcelona on Air Force One and met Prince Felipe of Spain, as well as Magic Johnson and Spike Lee. Even so, she considered herself "just an athlete . . . the same old kid, and someone who still wants to be one."

A month after the Winter Olympics, Kristi won the world championship for the second time in a row, the first American female skater to do so since Peggy Fleming in 1968. In September of 1992 she turned professional, which made her ineligible to compete in the 1993 World Championships. But a ruling passed during the summer of 1992 by the International Skating Union enabled her to apply for reinstatement as an amateur so she could qualify for the 1994 Winter Games in Lillehammer, Norway. She expressed uncertainty about going for the gold again, explaining in an interview, "Any medal would have made people happy in '92, but in '94 it will be expected to be gold. I've never had that kind of pressure on me before." She ultimately decided not to compete and was spared entanglement in the fray when the sport of ice-skating took a controversial turn with the scandal between two other Olympic contenders, Tonya Harding and Nancy Kerrigan.

Kristi's long-term goals include finishing college and raising a family. But in the meantime, she continues to ice-skate professionally and enjoy her other hobbies, which include tennis, rollerblading, and dancing.

Maya Lin stands on the site of the future Vietnam Veterans Memorial in Washington, D.C., shortly after her design for the memorial had been accepted.

Maya
Lin

MAYA YING LIN, THE SCULPTOR AND ARCHITECT BEST known for designing the Vietnam Veterans Memorial in Washington, D.C., was born on October 5, 1959, in Athens, Ohio. Her parents, Henry Huan Lin and Julia Chang Lin, immigrated to the United States during the 1940s and became, respectively, the dean of fine arts and a professor of literature at Ohio State University. Maya has one older brother, Tan Lin, who is a poet. Though her ancestors in China were prominent, including a progressive lawyer, a lyric poet, and a famous architect, Lin does not identify strongly with her Chinese heritage. She concedes that her work is "distinctly Asian" because of its simplicity and sense of introspection, and has stated that she responds more immediately to the Japanese aesthetic than the Western one. Another dichotomy is apparent in her work. As she once told an audience at the Metropolitan Museum of Art in 1990, "Architects call me a sculptor, and sculptors call me an architect."

Lin claims she was "somewhat of a nerd" during childhood. She spent most of her time playing by herself, building miniature towns in her room, reading, taking walks in the woods, playing chess with her brother, and throwing pots in her father's ceramics studio. In high school she didn't wear makeup or date, though she did have a part-time job at the local McDonald's, like any American teenager. She excelled in math, which helped shape her problem-solving approach to her work in architecture, but she also took college-level courses that introduced her to the existentialism of Jean-Paul Sartre and Albert Camus. She subsequently became somewhat preoccupied with the concept of death and pursued the subject while enrolled at Yale as an architecture major. In New Haven, Lin often visited the Grove Street

61

Cemetery to photograph the headstones, and when she went abroad for her junior year, she took the opportunity to visit European cemeteries. During her senior year Lin signed up for a course in funerary architecture, which proved pivotal for her subsequent career.

The class involved designing various monuments to death, "from a gateway to a cemetery to a memorial for World War III." A poster announced a competition for the Vietnam Veterans Memorial, and Lin's professor asked all the students to enter. The professor suggested that Lin visit the proposed monument site, which was in Washington, D.C., on the Mall between the Lincoln Memorial and the Capitol. As she photographed the site on a sunny November day in 1980, the basic idea for her eventually winning design came to her, "simply—not as a brainstorm," with the concept of opening the earth and evoking an apolitical serenity. It took her only two weeks to complete the series of pastel sketches that illustrated her design.

Lin's design for the memorial consisted of two long black granite walls that meet to form a slight V shape. The walls would be engraved with the names of the 58,156 killed or missing veterans of the Vietnam War, in the chronological order in which they died or disappeared. Rather than a "falsely heroic" statement about the war, Lin's design was a testament to her understanding that "war is not just a victory or loss," but about individual lives. Lin insisted on a chronological listing of the names because not only does each represent a moment in history, but as she explained, "People don't die in alphabetical order." The polished black stone, more "peaceful and gentle than white," acts like a kind of mirror, making viewers (or "mourners" as Lin says) see themselves as those among the living, and indicates an unseeable space, behind and beyond the walls, where the dead lie. One last element was vital, as Lin explained in the statement accompanying her competition entry: "As we turn to leave, we see these walls stretching into the distance, directing us to the Washington Monument, to the left, and the Lincoln Memorial, to the right, thus bringing the Vietnam memorial into historical context."

After five days of considering the 1,420 entries, the competition's judges declared Lin's entry, No. 1,026, the winner, calling it "superbly harmonious." Maya Lin was just 21 years old. The public announcement on May 6, 1981, was immediately met with protest by some veterans and their families. Some called it "a degrading ditch" and "a wall of shame," and even attacked Lin's Asian heritage, saying, "We can't have our memorial built by a gook." As Lin commuted weekly from New Haven to the nation's capital in the following months to oversee construction on the memorial, the protests and complaints only increased. H. Ross Perot, the right-wing conservative Texan who funded the design competition (and later ran for president in 1992), gathered irate veterans to demonstrate in Washington. Prominent attorney Tom Carhart called Lin's monument a memorial to "the war at home rather than the one in Southeast Asia." And former interior secretary James Watt even tried to deny the Vietnam memorial project a construction permit.

In early 1982 support arose for an alternative to Lin's monument. Sculptor and former antiwar demonstrator Frederick E. Hart had designed *The Three Servicemen Statue*, which had placed third in the competition. Protestors petitioned to have the bronze statue of three soldiers brandishing

Lin displays a model of the Vietnam Veterans Memorial. She was a 21-year-old Yale University architecture student when her design won the competition.

the American flag erected in the center of Lin's two-walled monument. Lin compared this proposal to "drawing mustaches on other people's portraits." In February 1982 a compromise was reached, calling for the erection of Hart's statue near the entrance to the memorial site, about 120 feet from Lin's wall. Lin received $20,000 in prize money from the Vietnam Veterans Memorial Fund, but the same fund gave Hart more than 10 times that amount for his commission. When the memorial was dedicated on November 13, 1982, the program depicted Hart's sculpture on its cover and neglected to mention Maya Lin's name at all during the ceremony. Her name appears only on a separate stone placed a few feet behind the memorial.

At the peak of the controversy, a group of prominent art critics gave their assessment of the memorial contest entries and reconfirmed that Lin's was in fact the best design. Today, her memorial is the most visited monument in Washington, seen by over a million people each year. She receives letters from veterans explaining how her memorial has helped them. One letter detailed how the healing process for patients

at a Pennsylvania clinic that treats Vietnam veterans trauma-
tized by the war culminates in a visit to the monument. And
every day the Park Service responsible for the site's upkeep
collects the flowers, photos, medals, and dog tags that veterans' friends and relatives leave as mementos at the base of the
wall.

Though her memorial has since been acknowledged
for its role in helping a country come to terms with its grief
over the Vietnam War, the storm of negative publicity had
its effect on Lin. She had received her M.F.A. in architecture
from Yale in 1981, and by the time of the dedication she was
enrolled in Harvard's Graduate School of Design. But the
press attention distracted her. She decided to take time off
from school and disappear from the limelight, becoming a
virtual recluse and even cutting her long hair very short. As
she later told reporters, she was "terrified that at 21 I might
already have outdone myself."

She spent most of 1983 working for an architecture
firm in Boston and returned to Yale that fall to finish graduate
school, studying with architect Frank Gehry. Before she
graduated in the spring of 1986, she had also contributed
sculpture to New York's Artpark and written about architecture for the *New Republic.* After graduation she set up a studio
in Manhattan's Lower East Side, out of which she planned to
work on architecture projects and sculpture. She lived with
two cats named Ranch and Trout and her male companion,
sculptor Peter Boynton, whom she had known since her
undergraduate years at Yale. She declined many invitations to
lecture, preferring to focus on the future. Though she had
resolved not to accept any more commissions for war memo-
rials, it wasn't long before she found herself involved with

designing one commemorating a different kind of war, the battle for racial equality.

In February 1988 Lin got a call from Edward Ashworth, a board member of the Southern Poverty Law Center (SPLC) in Montgomery, Alabama. The SPLC's executive director, Morris Dees, wanted Lin to design a monument dedicated to the people who had given their lives in the struggle for civil rights. The site of the memorial would be at the entrance plaza for the SPLC's new headquarters in Montgomery, the city where the bus boycotts of 1955–56 launched the modern era of civil rights protests. Lin accepted the project, surprised that there wasn't already a memorial to the civil rights movement.

Before flying down to Montgomery in May of that year, Lin did as much research as she could on the movement, including watching tapes of the PBS series "Eyes on the Prize." She read a transcript of Rev. Dr. Martin Luther King's "I Have a Dream" speech, given at the 1963 civil rights march on Washington. She knew her design for the civil rights memorial would be made out of black granite when she came to the line "With this faith we will be able to hew out of the mountain of despair a stone of hope." And when she read further to the words adapted from a biblical passage, "We will not be satisfied until justice rolls down like waters and righteousness like a mighty stream," she knew she had to somehow incorporate water into her design.

The resulting work consists of a black granite wall, about 9 feet tall and 39 feet long, engraved with the Martin Luther King quote beginning with "until justice rolls down like waters. . . ." In front of the wall rests a black granite disk measuring 12 feet across, inscribed with the names of 40 people who lost their lives in the civil rights struggle and the dates of 21 landmark events, listed chronologically around its perimeter. Separated by a noticeable space to suggest that the struggle is not yet over, the list begins with the Supreme Court's 1954 *Brown vs. Board of Education* decision outlawing segregation in schools and ends with Dr. King's assassination in 1968. A veil of water flows calmly over both pieces.

The November 5, 1989, dedication of the Civil Rights Memorial, attended by Rosa Parks and Martin Luther King III, among others, was an emotional one. Among those who cried in grief over lost loved ones were Mamie Till Mobley, whose son, Emmett Till, was killed in Mississippi in 1955 for allegedly whistling at a white woman; Mary Birchard, whose husband, William Moore, was murdered in Alabama in 1963 while protesting segregation; and the family of Willie Edwards, who was murdered by the Ku Klux Klan in Montgomery in 1957.

Lin's third commissioned monument, the *Women's Table,* was installed at Yale's main quadrangle in 1992 and commemorates the 100th anniversary of the first year that Yale admitted women into its graduate school. The work consists of a green granite oval tilted on its low bluestone base at a 69-degree angle, symbolizing 1969, the year female undergraduates were first admitted to Yale. The table's surface bears a spiral of numbers representing the number of women at Yale since its founding in 1701 up to 1991. Since women were barred for almost 200 years, the surface is filled with many zeros. Again, a curtain of water completes the piece.

Lin has also worked on other projects. She constructed a 4,000-square-foot house in Santa Monica, Califor-

Lin attends a meeting of the Washington Fine Arts Commission in 1982, where a controversy arose over placing a statue by Frederick Hart next to her memorial.

Maya Lin in her New York office in 1987.

nia, and renovated a Victorian townhouse in Connecticut. She designed a stage set in Philadelphia. She transformed the entranceway of the Charlotte Coliseum in North Carolina into a topiary park. She drew up Reginald Lewis's corporate logo, developed the open-air gathering place at Juniata College in Pennsylvania, and produced an environmental work of grass to grace the front of a Michigan aerospace company. When her father died in 1989, Lin set about drawing up plans for an addition to her childhood home in Ohio, where her mother still lives. In 1993 she finished remodeling loft space for the Museum of African Art in New York City.

During the fall of that year, Maya returned to her home state to install *Groundswell* at the Wexner Center for the Arts at Ohio State University. With a six-man crew and heavy construction equipment, Maya had 40 tons of green crushed glass, recycled from the Ford Motor Company, poured into three levels of outdoor space, forming gentle mounds reminiscent of a Japanese Zen garden. Maya did not expect any public criticism for this work, but unfortunately someone reacted with distaste for *Groundswell* by spilling red pigment over a large segment of it, enough to require the replacement of 14 tons of the crushed glass.

Maya's sixth public commission, a 38-foot-long elliptical clock for Pennsylvania Station in New York, should be less prone to vandalism. Her design for the clock was chosen from a competition as part of the Metropolitan Transportation Authority's Arts for Transit project. After five years in the making, the last part of which was spent at a Long Island foundry with a crew of 16 working on finishing the steel and aluminum, Maya's clock was installed in the summer of 1994. Maya hopes that hers will become as famous as the clock at the Biltmore Hotel. She wants to hear people say, "Meet me under the clock," and mean the one at Penn Station.

Despite her many architectural projects, Lin hasn't neglected her sculpture, for which she has received an NEA grant. She has exhibited her small-scale works, often hanging compositions of lead, beeswax, and broken glass, at the Sidney Janis Gallery, the Tibor de Nagy Gallery, and the Rosa Esman Gallery, all in New York. It seems that much of her career has been spent erecting grand-scale monuments, but as she told one interviewer, "I have to do the sculpture, too. Just doing one wouldn't be the full picture for me."

Isamu Noguchi at work in Tokyo, Japan, in 1950.

THE ABSTRACT MODERN SCULPTURE OF ISAMU NOGUCHI bridges not only the cultures of the East and West but also the worlds of fine and applied art. He worked in various media—brass, bronze, ceramics, steel, wood, and, most notably, stone. He was well known for his folding paper lamps (the *Akari*), for the stage sets he created for choreographers such as Martha Graham and George Balanchine, and for his groundbreaking abstract sculpture. In 1946 he was included in the Museum of Modern Art's exhibit *Fourteen Americans* and he received a Bollingen Foundation Fellowship in 1949 to research a book on leisure. He designed monuments, playgrounds, urban parks, furniture, and fountains and executed environmental projects, gardens, and corporate-sponsored public sculptures in cities across America, Japan, France, Italy, and Israel. He had retrospectives at the Whitney Museum of American Art in 1968 and at the Walker Art Center in Minneapolis in 1978. His representational portrait busts, from which he made his living in the early years of his career, were displayed at the National Portrait Gallery. He represented the United States at the 1986 Venice Biennale, and received the National Medal of Arts from President Ronald Reagan and the Third Order of the Sacred Treasure from the Japanese government. The Isamu Noguchi Garden Museum, located in Long Island City, N.Y., opened in May of 1985, documenting his 60-year career.

Isamu Noguchi was born on November 17, 1904, in Los Angeles, California. In 1893 his father, Yone Noguchi, had left Tokyo, where he had been a student at Keio University. He settled in San Francisco, where he became immersed in the poetry scene, and quickly achieved popularity as a poet in both America and England. In 1901 he met Isamu's mother,

Isamu Noguchi

Leonie Gilmour, a writer of Irish and American Indian heritage, who gave him editorial help. During their relationship Leonie became pregnant, but Yone left the country before Isamu was born, first stopping in London to promote his poetry, and then returning to Japan to become a professor of English at Keio University. In 1906 Leonie brought the two-year-old Isamu to Japan and lived in a house in Tokyo provided by Yone, who had by that time taken a Japanese wife. In his autobiography, *A Sculptor's World,* Isamu recalled an idyllic early childhood attending kindergarten and making his first sculpture, a sea wave made of clay and glazed in blue.

When Isamu was four his mother separated from his father and moved, taking Isamu with her to Chigasaki, a coastal village in Japan. They resided in a farmer's house for a few years, and Isamu lived like "a typical Japanese boy," going to the local school, making whistles out of twigs, fishing for eels, and enjoying the Japanese festivals. When Isamu was eight his mother had another child, a girl she named Ailes, and decided to have Isamu commute during the days to St. Joseph's College, a French Jesuit school in Yokohama. His mother wanted to live closer to the sea, and Isamu helped her build a house nearer the shores of Chigasaki. When Isamu turned 10, his mother took him out of school for a while and educated him at home, teaching him botany and sending him to a local carpenter to learn woodworking. Isamu learned how to use wood-carving tools and made traditional images in cherry wood. He also tended his first garden, in which he had installed a brook and planted rose bushes.

Isamu and his mother moved to Yokohama, where they lived in a Western-style house and Isamu, attending a "foreign" Catholic school, became "a foreigner myself, a stranger in the land." In 1917, when Isamu was 13, his mother decided that he "had better become completely American" to avoid any problems that he, a child of mixed parentage, might have being accepted in Japanese society. She read a magazine article about the Interlaken School in northern Indiana and decided to send Isamu there. In July of the following year Isamu said goodbye to Japan and boarded the boat that would take him to America, alone. Ironically, his father, himself a product of Western education, appeared at the dock to try to stop Isamu from leaving; apparently Yone, who had been a cultural bridge between East and West through his poetry and writings in English about Japanese art, had been overcome by feelings of nationalism during World War I (1914–18). But Isamu's mother was determined to send the teenage Isamu abroad. He arrived safely at the school in the Indiana countryside.

The school, however, did not open in the fall. It had been converted into an army training camp, and since Isamu's mother couldn't afford to send him anywhere else, he stayed there through the winter, even after the Armistice on November 11, 1918. He took shelter with two caretakers in a deserted building on the school grounds and would ride out on a horse before dawn to retrieve mail and food. He eventually began attending public school in nearby Rolling Prairie.

The next summer the founder of the Interlaken School, Dr. Edward A. Rumley, "rescued" Isamu from his rough existence and took him to LaPorte, Indiana, where he was sent to live with Dr. Rumley's friend, a minister named Dr. Samuel Mack. While attending high school for the next three years (under the name "Sam Gilmour"), Isamu helped earn his keep by mowing lawns and delivering newspapers, all

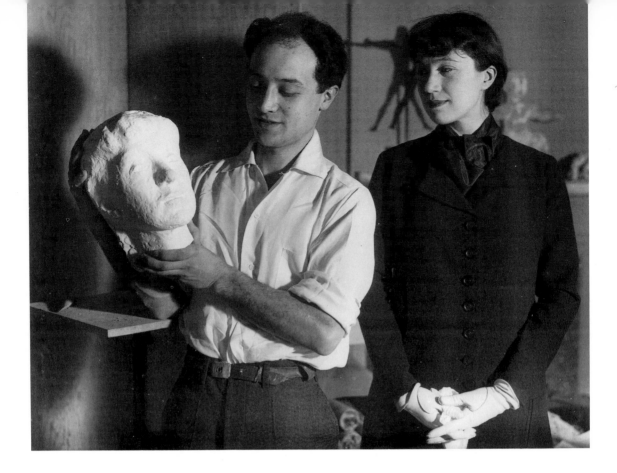

Noguchi with his bust of the dancer Agna Enters in New York in 1932.

the while worrying about his mother in Japan—and resenting his father.

After high school graduation, Isamu announced to Dr. Rumley that he wanted to become an artist. Dr. Rumley thought it would be better for Isamu to become a doctor but arranged for him to apprentice with another of his friends, the sculptor Gutzon Borglum, whose well-known carving of the faces of former U.S. presidents into Mount Rushmore was at that time only an idea. Isamu stayed with Borglum in his home near Stamford, Connecticut, and helped work on Borglum's war memorial in Newark, New Jersey, getting horses to pose and posing on a horse himself as General Sherman. Isamu didn't do much sculpting, but he did learn how to cast plaster. At the end of the apprenticeship, Borglum informed Isamu that he would never be a sculptor.

So Isamu decided to become a doctor after all and, in January 1923, enrolled at Columbia University, receiving tuition assistance from his benefactor, Dr. Rumley, and taking a night job in a restaurant to make ends meet. While studying premedicine, Isamu made the acquaintance of the famous bacteriologist Dr. Hideyo Noguchi, who had known Isamu's father, but was not related. The bacteriologist told Isamu that he should become an artist, since not everyone was gifted enough to become a doctor.

While Isamu was deciding what to do, his mother had finally returned to America. She settled in Greenwich Village, where she had been born. Isamu went to live with her, though by this time he felt less emotionally attached, since he hadn't seen her for many years. Isamu, who had still been using his mother's last name, decided to change his last name to his father's, even though he felt "completely American" with "no hint" of Japan about him. His name change accompanied his conscious decision to become a sculptor and reflected a perhaps subconscious pull from his roots in Japan.

When Isamu was 19, his mother happened to notice the Leonardo da Vinci Art School on the Lower East Side and suggested he check it out. At first Isamu was disdainful of the academic stonecutting school, and when the director, Onorio Ruotolo, asked if he wanted to study there, Isamu told him he "wasn't interested in sculpture." Ruotolo offered Isamu a scholarship after he made a copy of a foot in plaster, and Isamu attended the school in the evenings, almost reluctantly. He tried to stop going to the art school with the excuse that he went to college and worked nights in a restaurant. But Ruotolo offered to pay Isamu the equivalent of what he earned at the restaurant so he could quit that job. As Isamu puts it in his autobiography, "How could I resist? I became a sculptor, even against my will."

Within three months Isamu held his first one-man exhibit at the Leonardo da Vinci Art School. He stopped going to classes at Columbia and became immersed in what he later described as the "slick and quick way of doing academic sculpture." He was elected to the National Sculpture Society and had regular exhibitions with the National Academy and the Architectural League, but soon he became disenchanted with academic art and widened his horizons to embrace the world of international modern art.

In 1926 he began frequenting exhibitions of modern art, particularly in the galleries of the photographer Alfred Stieglitz and J. B. Neuman, who took Isamu under his wing. Isamu saw an exhibit by the sculptor Constantin Brancusi and was "transfixed by his vision." That year he applied for the then newly founded Guggenheim Fellowship, with which he intended to undertake three years of production and travel, first to Paris, then to Asia, including India, China, and Japan. "It is my desire to view nature through nature's eyes," he wrote in his application, "and to ignore man as an object for special veneration. . . . My father, Yone Noguchi, is Japanese and has long been known as an interpreter of the East to the West, through poetry. I wish to do the same with sculpture."

In 1927 Isamu received the fellowship and arrived in Paris by April of that year. By sheer chance, someone overheard him mention Brancusi and introduced him to the famous sculptor, who agreed to let him work as his studio assistant beginning the very next day. For the next few months Isamu spent half of every day with Brancusi, learning to use stoneworking tools and communicating through glance and gesture, since Brancusi spoke no English and Isamu no French. Isamu made some attempt at preparing for the next leg of travel he had outlined in his fellowship and went briefly to London to research Oriental art at the British Museum Library, but when his fellowship was renewed for the following year, he decided that all he wanted to do was make sculpture. He moved to a studio outside Paris, in Gentilly, and set to work. He made numerous abstract sculptures in stone, wood,

Isamu Noguchi
in 1971.

and sheet metal, which were exhibited at the Eugene Shoen Gallery upon his return to New York. Because of his lapse in fulfilling his travel itinerary, he failed to have his fellowship renewed for a third year.

In New York Isamu was forced to find a way to make a living. None of his sculptures at the Shoen Gallery had sold, despite a favorable review in the *New York Times.* So Isamu began making portrait busts or "heads," as he referred to them. He described making heads as "a very good way of getting to know people" and made lifelong friends of the choreographer Martha Graham and the scientist Buckminster Fuller this way. His portrait busts were exhibited at Marie Sterner's gallery, the Harvard Society of Contemporary Art, and the Arts Club in Chicago. By the spring of 1930 Isamu had made enough money to resume his plan of travel.

Stopping first in Paris, Isamu intended to reach Japan via the Trans-Siberian Railroad. But in July he received a letter from his father telling him not to come to Japan using Noguchi as his name. Isamu decided to go to Beijing, China, instead, where he lived comfortably for eight months and studied brush-drawing with the acclaimed painter Chi Pai Shi.

In 1931 Isamu decided to go to Japan, intending to make only a brief visit and then return to China. He stayed for seven months, two in Tokyo visiting his father and the remainder in Kyoto, where he worked with the potter Jim-matsu Unou. He was inspired by the Zen gardens of Japan and created some terra-cotta sculptures, which were shown along with his China brush-drawings in New York upon his return in the fall of 1932.

Though he had several exhibitions throughout the spring of 1933, none of his works sold, and he was evicted from his studio. His affluent friends helped him find shelter in the posh Hotel des Artistes. Struck by the contrast between poverty and luxury, he became more socially conscious and developed friendships with like-minded artists. He decided he wanted to create sculpture that was "at once abstract and socially relevant." With this in mind, he began designing ideas for outdoor public spaces, such as *Play Mountain,* a giant playground to be built somewhere in Manhattan, and *Monument to the Plow,* a steel plow placed atop a huge triangular pyramid about a mile wide at each base and positioned in the geographical center of the United States. These ideas were never realized—one critic even called them "wily"—but they represented to Isamu important ideals. The monument was his "wish to belong to America, to its vast horizons of earth," and the playground was "the kernel out of which have grown all my ideas relating sculpture to the earth."

In 1934 his choreographer friend, Martha Graham, asked him to do his first set for her modern-dance stage performance *Frontier.* In 1935 the WPA (Works Progress Administration) had been established, and Isamu applied to the arts section to get funding. But he was consistently refused on the basis that he could make money by making heads, though he suspected that he had alienated the WPA New York arts director by doing an unflattering bust of her. So in 1936 Isamu went to Hollywood and raised money for a trip to Mexico by making heads. He found it refreshing that artists were "useful people, a part of the community" in Mexico and stayed for nearly a year, completing his first major work, a 22-meter-long mural he called *History of Mexico.*

Isamu was back in New York in 1937, doing heads again for money. He entered competitions and dabbled in

Isamu Noguchi stands before his 30-feet-high doughnut-shaped
fountain at Detroit's Civic Center in 1979.

industrial design. In 1938 he won a design competition for the plaque above the Associated Press building in Rockefeller Center, which took him over a year to execute, using about nine tons of stainless steel. Soon after that, the events of World War II began to put a damper on his artistic activities.

In 1942 Isamu became active in trying to "counteract the bigoted hysteria" that affected Japanese Americans, forming a group called Nisei Writers and Artists for Democracy. In Washington he met John Collier of the American Indian Service, who asked his help in developing park and recreation areas for the Indian territory that was a planned site for the internment of Japanese Americans under Executive Order Number 9066. Isamu spent months in the harsh conditions of the Poston, Arizona, internment camp, establishing a sense of solidarity with the Japanese American internees, even though his stay was voluntary. He remained for over seven months, but his plans for the camp's landscape were never carried out. As he related in his autobiography, his experience affected him deeply: "Freedom earned has a quality of assurance. The deep depression that comes with living under a cloud of suspicion, which we as Nisei experienced, lifted, and was followed by tranquility. I was free finally of causes. . . . I resolved henceforth to be an artist only." Isamu continued to fulfill his resolution until his death in New York on December 30, 1988.

Anna May Wong.

ONE OF THE MOST FAMOUS ACTRESSES OF HER TIME, Anna May Wong was also the first Asian American actress to achieve worldwide stardom. Her career spanned four decades, and though opportunities were scarce in Hollywood for actors of Asian descent to play substantial roles, Anna May appeared in over 50 movies, imbuing each character with a unique appeal.

Anna May Wong was born on January 3, 1907, in Los Angeles, California. Her Cantonese given name, Wong Liu Tsong, means "frosted yellow willow." Her family lived on Flower Street in the Chinatown district, where her father ran a laundry. As a young girl, on evenings when she was supposed to attend Chinese school, Anna May would sneak out to the nickelodeons, movies so-called because of their five-cent admission price. She loved watching Crane Wilbur and Pearl White, who starred in a series of nickelodeons called "The Perils of Pauline."

In 1919 Anna May met James Wang, a Hollywood agent who specialized in hiring "Oriental" talent. During that time, and throughout the 1920s and 1930s, when a Hollywood movie called for an "Oriental" role the industry used mainly Caucasian actors and actresses, heavily made up in a technique now referred to as "yellow-facing," after a similar practice used on white actors playing black roles. One Asian American actor, Sessue Hayakawa, had already begun to make a name for himself in 1914, but it would be years before Anna May would achieve stardom, eventually replacing the Caucasian actress Myrna Loy, who at that time seemed Hollywood's favorite choice to play Asian female roles.

But for now Wang cast the 12-year-old Anna May as an extra in *The Red Lantern*, a Nazimova film about the Boxer

Anna May Wong

Rebellion in turn-of-the-century China. Anna May was hired to play a lantern carrier in one scene in the movie. When the film debuted in Los Angeles in April 1919, a group of Chinese children attended the film, anxiously anticipating catching a glimpse of their fellow Chinatown resident. Unfortunately, they were disappointed; when the awaited scene began to unfold on the big screen, the young Anna May was hidden from view among the 300 other lantern bearers standing closely together.

Anna May continued to take obscure roles as an extra in a few more films, including *First Born*, with Sessue Hayakawa, and *Dinty*, starring Colleen Moore. Anna May's father opposed her new hobby. He was extremely overprotective of her, making sure that an adult always accompanied her to the studio. Sometimes he even locked her in her room if he discovered that a movie she was in had no other Asians in the cast. But the budding actress would not be discouraged.

In 1921, at age 14, Anna May played her first role of substance, for which she received billing in the movie credits. The movie was *Bits of Life*, directed by Marshal Nielan. As an anthology film, the first of its kind, *Bits of Life* was comprised of four episodes. One story line was original, written by the director, and the others were based on popular magazine pieces. In the segment entitled "Hop," Anna May played the daughter of an aging San Francisco Chinatown man, played by Lon Chaney, who is torn between the cultures of the old country and the new.

Two years later, in 1923, 16-year-old Anna May took the lead role in *Toll of the Sea*, one of the first Technicolor movies, with a plot similar to that of the classic *Madame Butterfly*. She finished the year with supporting roles in two other films, *Drifting* and *Thundering Dawn*, both released by Universal. In 1924 Anna May landed her second major role. The movie was called *The Thief of Bagdad*. As that year's big Douglas Fairbanks production, the movie got a lot of attention, as did 17-year-old Anna May, who wore a skimpy but glamorous costume while playing the princess's Mongolian slave.

Anna May went on to complete two Paramount pictures directed by Herbert Brenon that year. She played an Eskimo in *The Alaskan*, with Thomas Meighan and Estelle Taylor, and she had a supporting role as Tiger Lily, an Indian

As an actress, Wong had difficulty avoiding the roles that cast her as the stereotypical mysterious Oriental seductress.

chieftainess, in *Peter Pan*, which starred Betty Bronson. *Peter Pan* was, incidentally, filmed by Asian American cinematographer James Wong Howe, who went on to achieve his own degree of notoriety in the filmmaking world. That year, Anna May also appeared in the 10-episode movie serial *The Fortieth Door*.

The following year, 1925, she made only one film, Paramount's *Forty Winks*, starring Raymond Griffith, with Anna May, at a mere 18 years old, playing a sexy vamp. For the remainder of the year she filled her surplus time by working as a model for fur coat makers in the Los Angeles area. By that time, she had already grown to her full adult height of five feet, seven inches.

In 1926 her career picked up again. She took roles in four movies, including *The Desert's Toll*, *Fifth Avenue*, and *A Trip to Chinatown*, though none of them merited much attention. The next year was busier still: she appeared in six movies, including Warner Brothers' *Old San Francisco*, MGM's *Mr. Wu*, Chadwick Productions' *Driven from Home*, Tiffany's *Streets of Shanghai* (with a young Jason Robards), and two United Artists releases, *The Devil Dancer* and *The Dove*. In *Mr. Wu*, Anna May again played opposite Lon Chaney.

In 1928 Anna May topped her record with seven more films. Of note were *The Chinese Parrot*, the second Charlie Chan feature, directed by German expatriate Paul Leni; *Across to Singapore*, featuring Joan Crawford and James Mason; and *The Crimson City*, which starred Myrna Loy playing the Asian female lead, but featured Anna May in only a supporting role.

At that point Anna May became a bit disillusioned by Hollywood's reluctance to cast Asian actors in the lead parts of the "Oriental dramas" that were becoming so popular then.

She traveled to Europe in 1929, spending the next few years performing in film and theater productions. In England she appeared in E. A. Dupont's *Piccadilly*, a film featuring at least one other actor of Asian descent, King Ho-Chang, as well as Charles Laughton and Gilda Gray.

Anna May's stage debut took place at the New Theatre in London. With the beautiful young actress especially in mind, Basil Dean, a former actor turned director, bought a Chinese play called *Circle of Chalk* and cast Anna May in the lead opposite a young rising talent named Laurence Olivier. While in England, Anna May also appeared in both the theater and film versions of *On the Spot*, a highly successful Edgar Wallace thriller, in which she played a gangster's mistress. She also played a part in *Elstree Calling*, a 1930 British International release directed in part by Alfred Hitchcock.

Anna May ventured across the Continent, where she reprised her roles in the French and German versions of her British films, having become fluent in both of those languages. Afterward she took a turn behind the scenes, producing a play called *Tschun-Tshi* (Springtime), which ran successfully in Vienna, Austria.

By 1931 *On the Spot* had made it to Broadway back in the States, and the actress returned to play her role of the gangster's mistress. After seven and a half months she moved back to Hollywood to do a movie for Paramount called *Daughter of the Dragon*, which also featured Sessue Hayakawa. In this film, Anna took the role of Fu Manchu's daughter, playing her as an "Oriental temptress," the image Anna May became most noted for.

But perhaps her next role was her best. In the 1932 Paramount picture *Shanghai Express*, directed by Josef von

Another studio shot of Anna May Wong in costume.

Sternberg, Anna May's smoldering Parisian character holds her own against Marlene Dietrich's Shanghai Lily as she thwarts the career of a Chinese warlord played by Warner Oland. Anna May did a Sherlock Holmes movie next, 1933's *Study in Scarlet*, with Reginald Owen playing the clever detective.

After that Anna May moved back to England for nearly three years, appearing in such films as *Limehouse Blues* and *Java Head*, as well as performing on radio, where she took part in the King George Jubilee Program in 1935. She also traveled around Scotland, Ireland, and the outlying British provinces with a vaudeville troupe.

In 1936 Anna May visited the land of her ancestors for the first and only time. During a brief stopover in Japan, reporters asked Anna about her love life and whether she had any serious male friends. "No," she told them. "I am wedded to my art." The next day, the newspapers carried stories saying that she had married a man named Art. In fact, however, Anna May stayed single for her whole life.

A mob of adoring fans met her arrival in China's capital, then referred to as Peiping. She had a wonderful time during her eight months abroad, writing articles about her travels for American newspapers such as the *New York Herald Tribune*. In China she studied Mandarin and bought costumes to wear on stage and in films. Later she auctioned off those costumes, as well as some of her jewelry, and donated the money to the Chinese War Relief.

When she returned to the States in 1937, she starred in Paramount's *Daughter of Shanghai*, with Anthony Quinn playing the role of a gangster. In an annoying distraction later that year, Anna May received a number of letters threatening to

Anna May Wong in 1934, photographed upon her return to the United States from England, where she had worked in several British film productions.

injure her and her father if she refused to help finance a certain movie. Another actor, David Selznick, also received threatening letters, which were traced to a religious fanatic before any harm was done.

In 1938 Anna May was again featured with Anthony Quinn in Paramount's *Dangerous To Know,* and also put in a performance in Warner Brothers' *When Were You Born?* She tried out for the parts of both first and second wife in the big MGM production of Pearl Buck's *The Good Earth,* but after several readings and screen tests, she was passed over. It was a great disappointment for her, and a bit of a turning point, because she never had the chance to perform in a work of that quality again.

She finished out the rest of her contract with Paramount in 1939, appearing in two more movies with Anthony

Quinn, *Island of Lost Men* and *King of Chinatown*. She also did radio shows such as "The Mercury Theatre" and "The Edgar Bergen Show," and traveled with her stage act as far as Australia. In 1940 she signed with Columbia Pictures to do *Ellery Queen's Penthouse Mystery* with Ralph Bellamy. In 1942 she was scheduled to do three movies for Producer's Releasing Corp., but only two, *Bombs over Burma* and *The Lady from Chunking*, were actually made. The low quality of those films discouraged Anna from acting until after the war, during which she participated in USO activities and helped the Chinese War Relief.

In 1949 she did the suspense thriller *Impact* for United Artists before turning to television work. In 1951 Anna May starred in her own television series, "The Gallery of Madame Liu Tsong." She played the owner of an international chain of art galleries, who solved crimes and mysteries in her leisure time. The show aired on the Dumont Network and had a short run of only 11 episodes. Over the next few years, Anna May played parts in a number of other television dramas on the major networks.

In 1960 Anna May completed the last two films of her career. Anthony Quinn starred in both movies, along with Lana Turner in Universal's *Portrait in Black* and Peter O'Toole in Paramount's *The Savage Innocents*. The following year, Anna May's career was cut short. While preparing for a part in the film version of *Flower Drum Song*, she had been staying at the Santa Monica home of her photographer brother, Richard. On February 3, 1961, Anna May died of a heart attack in her sleep.

CRITICS HAIL YO-YO MA AS THE WORLD'S FINEST CEL-
LIST. He has won eight Grammy awards and is an exclusive
Sony Classical recording artist. His musical repertoire consists
of playing solo concerts, recitals with piano, ensemble chamber music, and teaching. His long-standing partnership with
the pianist Emanuel Ax is known as one of the most successful
in the classical music world. He has played both classical and
contemporary compositions in hundreds of concerts the
world over with the finest orchestras and musicians, and he
still finds time each touring season to devote to educating
young musicians. He teaches master classes and engages in
informal discussions with student audiences. The 1989 docu-
mentary *Yo-Yo Ma: A Month at Tanglewood* was made about his
experiences with students at the Tanglewood Music Center,
where he spends part of every summer. He helped organize
the Committee of 100, a leadership resource group of distinguished Chinese Americans, including the architect I. M. Pei
and General Motors vice president Shirley Young, who represent the interests of the Chinese American community. His
current instruments of choice are a Montagnana cello made
in 1733 and a Davidoff Stradivarius made in 1712.

Yo-Yo Ma was born in Paris on October 7, 1955, to
Hiao-Tsiun and Marina Ma. His father is from Ningbo, a
city south of Shanghai in China, and his mother is from Hong
Kong. Yo-Yo Ma's parents met at China's Nanjing University, where Hiao-Tsiun was a professor and Marina a student
in his music theory class. In 1936 Hiao-Tsiun, like many
educated Chinese, left the country after the government under
Chiang Kai-Shiek had made the society increasingly unstable.
Hiao-Tsiun moved to Paris and continued his study of music.

Marina followed in 1949; they married, and she gave birth to Yo-Yo Ma's older sister, Yeou-Cheng, two years later. In Chinese, "Yo" means "friendship," and is a derivation of the character for his father's name, "Ma," which means "horse." Yo-Yo Ma and his sister each have the "Yo" character in their names, according to Chinese custom, and Yo-Yo Ma jokingly attributes his second "Yo" to laziness on the part of his parents.

Hiao-Tsiun, who later founded the Children's Orchestra in New York and whom Yo-Yo describes as "a born pedagogue," passed on his love of education and music to his children, teaching them subjects ranging from French history to calligraphy and having them learn to play classical instruments. During their early childhood in Paris, Yeou-Cheng studied the violin and Yo-Yo began learning the piano and cello. When he was just four years old, Yo-Yo astonished his cello teacher, Michelle Lepinte, by learning to play one of Bach's Suites for Unaccompanied Cello. Hiao-Tsiun had taught Yo-Yo that Bach would "assuage fear, loneliness, and hunger" and assigned the budding prodigy two measures of Bach to memorize every day. By breaking up a long and dense Bach suite into manageable segments, Yo-Yo was able to *coupez la difficulté en quatre* (cut the difficulty by four), a principle Yo-Yo found helpful because he admittedly did not like to work hard. In this manner, Yo-Yo avoided the stress often experienced by young cellists. As he explained in an article in the *New Yorker* magazine, "When a problem is complex, you become tense, but when you break it down into basic components you can approach each element without stress. Then, when you put it all together, you do something that seems externally complex, but you don't feel it that way." By age five

Yo-Yo had learned three Bach suites. At that tender age, he also gave his first public recital, playing both piano and a scaled-down cello, at the University of Paris.

The Ma family visited New York in 1962, when Hiao-Tsiun's brother, who had recently immigrated, was experiencing some difficulty in America. Hiao-Tsiun convinced his brother to stay, and the Mas ended up staying themselves. Yo-Yo resumed his music study under the cellist Janos Scholz. When Yo-Yo was nine, Isaac Stern, the distinguished violinist who had seen him play in Paris and had already recognized his extraordinary talent, arranged for him to study with Leonard Rose, under whose tutelage he flourished, despite the intensity of endless memorization that comes with the study of classical music. As a child, it was Yo-Yo's love of music that kept him going; one particular favorite was the Schubert E-Flat-Major Trio, in recordings by greats such as Pablo Casals. Rose, then a man in his fifties, was a feisty character who sometimes coaxed Yo-Yo out of his shyness by urging him to "Sock it to me, baby!"

Growing up in America, Yo-Yo experienced many of the problems typical in families whose parents were raised in a different culture. The Mas spoke Chinese at home and went to Chinese movies to teach the children traditional values. But Yo-Yo considered himself American and also learned American values. Because he couldn't disobey his parents at home, he rebelled at school. He started cutting classes in the fifth grade and habitually did so throughout high school. After he was enrolled in the Professional Children's School in New York in 1968, his truancy led teachers to conclude that he was simply bored. He was put in an accelerated program, and he graduated at the age of 15.

As conductor John Williams applauds in the background, Yo-Yo Ma receives congratulations from another musician at the conclusion of a Boston Pops concert in 1988.

He spent the summer after high school graduation away from home, attending Ivan Galamian's camp for string players at Meadowmount in the Adirondacks, where he let loose a bit with his newfound freedom and even got caught painting a wall with graffiti. His youthful exuberance translated to his music, and he played more passionately than he ever had before. It was the beginning of a phase of typical adolescent rebellion in Yo-Yo's life, but one which had beneficial effects on his music.

By the time Yo-Yo resumed music lessons with Leonard Rose in the fall, he had added a leather jacket to his wardrobe and four-letter words to his vocabulary. Rose took the change in Yo-Yo's behavior in stride and gave him leeway to begin to explore his own musical path, which can be one of the most difficult things a teacher can do. That year, Yo-Yo gave his first recital in New York at Carnegie Recital Hall.

Yo-Yo's sister, Yeou-Cheng, had been attending Radcliffe, and Yo-Yo thought about applying to Harvard, but at 15, he felt too young to leave home again. He enrolled at Columbia University, continued his lessons with Rose at Juilliard, and lived with his parents. The combination of challenging music study, high-caliber academics, and natural growing pains took their toll. Yo-Yo dropped out of Columbia and didn't tell his parents. He spent his time at Juilliard, making the usual teenage attempts at peer acceptance by getting a fake I.D. and drinking heavily, even during rehearsals. One day he passed out from the effects of alcohol and was taken to the hospital. His parents feared that he was becoming an alcoholic, while Rose worried that he was under too much pressure and suggested that he see a psychiatrist.

Yo-Yo's teenage antics did not seriously affect his music career. The next year, when he was 16, he performed at the Marlboro Festival in Vermont with more experienced artists such as Felix Galimer, Isidore Cohen, and Sándor Végh, and played in the orchestra under the direction of Pablo Casals, the cello master to whom Yo-Yo is now often compared. Yo-Yo spent the next three summers performing at Marlboro.

When Yo-Yo was 17, he decided he was ready to try again at combining music and academic study. He could have pursued a full-time career in classical music, but he decided that to forego a college education would preclude his development as a well-rounded human being. He attended Harvard, studying music as well as history, anthropology, literature, and natural sciences. These subjects offered him ways to understand the diverse influences in his life—his Chinese heritage, growing up in Paris, and moving to America. He began to put elements of his childhood in perspective and appreciate the vast cultural variety that exists in humankind.

Yo-Yo studied chamber music with Leon Kirchner, who taught him to look at pieces from a composer's point of view. He also gained from his associations with Luise Vosgerchian and Patricia Zander, both pianists and former students of Nadia Boulanger. At Harvard, Yo-Yo learned how to analyze a musical score and understand how a composition works to sustain the listener's interest. This contributed to his appreciation of the composer and to his attitude that composers and performers should influence each other for mutual benefit. In his later involvement with the Massachusetts Council on the Arts and Humanities, Yo-Yo worked toward fulfilling his ideal by commissioning works from the community of contemporary composers.

While still at Harvard, Yo-Yo debuted in London with the Royal Philharmonic Orchestra. He performed more and more frequently and realized he could make a living as a classical cellist. He considered leaving the university, but his father persuaded him to stay and, to prevent his career from affecting his studies, advised Yo-Yo to perform concerts only once a month.

Throughout his years at Harvard, Yo-Yo was also cultivating a relationship with Jill Hornor, who would later become his wife. Yo-Yo first met Jill during a spring concert he gave at Mount Holyoke, where Jill was a student. They met again during Yo-Yo's first summer at Marlboro, where Jill happened to be working, and by the end of the festival Yo-Yo had fallen in love. He corresponded with Jill throughout her junior year in Paris, her final year at Mount Holyoke, and her

Carnegie Hall, 1991. From left to right, violinist Isaac Stern, Yo-Yo Ma, and conductor Zubin Mehta.

years of graduate study at Cornell. Finally, in 1977 Yo-Yo asked Jill to marry him, and she accepted. At first Yo-Yo's father was upset by the engagement; he was afraid his son's marriage to a Westerner would result in a disintegration of their traditional Chinese family values, but he eventually accepted the situation and welcomed Jill as his daughter-in-law. Yo-Yo and Jill spent three years at Harvard's Leverett House, where he was artist-in-residence, before buying a house in Winchester, Massachusetts. They have two children, Nicholas and Emily, to whom Yo-Yo's father has also given Chinese names.

In 1980, when Yo-Yo was 24, he underwent an operation for scoliosis, a curvature of his spine that may have been exacerbated by his cello playing. If the operation had not succeeded, he might have been prevented from playing again, and he had prepared himself for that possibility. In previous years he had gone through periods of unhappiness, questioning whether his hectic concert schedule impaired his development as a person and whether he might be happier living a more normal life, perhaps as a teacher. But the operation was a success and the straightening of his spine even resulted in an additional two inches to his height. He realized that he is truly happy to fulfill his destiny as a performing cellist and valued his normal life—his wife and kids—as important to the preservation of his well-being as an artist.

Yo-Yo sees himself as "just a performing musician" and believes the highest peak of performing is reached not when the audience is just listening to the musician's technique, but when the audience is truly in contact with the message the music is sending—when "a composer's ideas from two hundred years ago find absolute contact in their purest form with people living now." He feels he is the medium through which the composer's ideas are translated. "I know my greatest joy as a musician when I am playing a concert dedicated exclusively to Bach," he once said. "For a whole evening I'm living in one man's mind—a great man's mind. That's how I can justify being a performer. One is involved in a process that is larger than oneself." It's easy to see why Yo-Yo Ma has earned an international reputation as an ambassador for classical music by breaking down its elitist image, as these preconcert remarks he once made in Monte Carlo illustrate: "When I give a concert, I like to think that I'm welcoming someone to my home. I've lived with the music for a long time; it's an old friend and I want to say, 'Let's all participate.'"

Margaret Cho, star of "All American Girl," the first
television situation comedy about an Asian American family.

MARGARET CHO IS THE STAR OF THE FIRST TELEVISION sitcom whose central character is an Asian American woman. She originally trained to be an actress before drifting into the realm of stand-up comedy, where her semiautobiographical riffs have found a more receptive audience. Her act is a combination of memories of growing up in the culturally vapid 1980s and anecdotes about twentysomethings living in the 1990s, but Margaret also deals with issues such as racism and generational conflict—all to very humorous effect.

Margaret was born in San Francisco in 1969. Her grandfather was a Methodist minister who managed an orphanage in Seoul during the Korean War. Her parents, both first-generation Korean Americans, raised Margaret in a liberal yet traditional household. Her father, Seung Hoon Cho, writes jokes for the Korean market. According to Margaret, his books have titles like "1,001 Jokes for Public Speakers—real corny stuff." Apparently, Margaret's comic sensibility was not inherited. "We never laugh at each other's jokes," she often tells reporters. "I just don't understand them."

Margaret was never the class clown in school. She considered herself "sort of a typical Asian American kid, studious, somewhat shy, somewhat reserved." But her early years became a rich source for much of her current stand-up comedy material. For example, she was obsessed with television. "Those are my icons," she explained in a magazine interview, "anybody that was on television between 1974 and 1984. I would love to be like a Pamela Des Barres type. But not I'm With the Band, but I'm With the Cast of Three's Company." In her stand-up routine, she recalls how she used to play "Charlie's Angels" as a kid. To reenact the scenes where the bad guys would use chloroform to knock someone out, Margaret and her girlfriends would use "a sock and nail polish remover. We'd be out cold."

She confesses to having been "a hard-core Duran-ie in 1983–84" and laments the fact that Duran Duran's lead singer, Simon Le Bon, hasn't aged well. "He looks like Shirley Maclaine," she quips. Margaret claims to have been one of the first Madonna wannabes, complete with black rubber bangles encircling both forearms. Years later she got the opportunity to meet with Madonna and took a tour of her office. "I sat at her desk, and I twirled around, and picked up the phone . . . I was so excited." Afterward Madonna gave her a T-shirt with the words, "Love, Madonna." But Margaret won't wear it. "Somebody would think that I wrote it."

As a child Margaret took voice, dance, and piano lessons, all with her parents' approval. But at age 13, when she started showing an interest in children's theater, her parents began to withhold their encouragement. Margaret's growing propensity for the dramatic would not be easily dampened, however. She auditioned for the High School of the Performing Arts in San Francisco and, rendering the part of Ophelia from Shakespeare's *Hamlet*, was admitted.

But being Asian American was something of a hindrance in the field of acting. "I was never the star of any productions," she says. "I was always the Danny Aiello type." In 1988 she entered the theater program at San Francisco State University, hoping to continue her acting studies at Juilliard or Yale. But her frustration with the limited roles available to Asian actors led her to try another field of entertainment she had never considered before—comedy.

A comedy club called the Rose and Thistle was built above the bookstore that Margaret's parents owned. Margaret worked at the bookstore part-time and began frequenting the club with her friends, who eventually talked her into taking the mike on amateur nights. Margaret's act developed, and soon she was doing stand-up regularly, running upstairs to perform during breaks at her parents' bookstore. She doesn't remember much about what her comedy routine was like then. She didn't prepare anything, but just went on stage and talked about whatever was going on in her life. As a young stand-up playing the San Francisco comedy clubs such as the Improv, the Punchline, and Holy City Zoo, Margaret was very well received by everyone except her parents, who, she says, were "less than thrilled." They even tried to schedule her to work the bookstore at night so she couldn't go to the clubs.

One person who did encourage Margaret was Jerry Seinfeld, the now-famous comedian who stars on his own television show, *Seinfeld.* In 1991 Margaret and Seinfeld shared the bill at the U.S. College Comedy Competition at Daytona Beach. Margaret had been named West Coast division champion, and Seinfeld praised the uniqueness of her act.

In 1992 Margaret dropped out of college and relocated to Los Angeles to pursue a career in comedy full-time. Her parents were extremely upset. "I let comedy sort of take over everything in my life," she told a magazine interviewer. She characterizes the failure to complete a formal education as "the worst thing you can do if you're in an Asian family. That's just worse than suicide or standing on a water tower and killing lots of people. At least mass murder can be justified if you have some sort of a college degree." Margaret experi-

Margaret's first effort at
stand-up comedy came at The
Rose & Thistle, a comedy
club that opened above the
San Francisco bookstore
owned by her parents.

enced a falling-out with her parents, and for the next few years they did not speak to each other.

During her early days of touring, Margaret would perform "in anything, like biker bars, barbecues, roadside truck stops, bad, bad places to perform in." But within a year after her move to L.A., clips of her act began showing up on television. She appeared on A&E's "Evening at the Improv,"

Fox's "Comic Strip Live," MTV's "Half-Hour Comedy Hour," and VH-I's "Comedy Spotlight." She was featured on the Lifetime channel's "Six Comics in Search of a Generation" and later shared the stage with comedian Bobby Collins on Showtime's "A Pair of Jokers." She has appeared on talk shows including "Arsenio Hall" and "The Dennis Miller Show," and has even given voice to a cartoon character, on the animated series "Itsy Bitsy Spider."

When she appeared on NBC's "Bob Hope Presents the Ladies of Laughter," her parents, who happened to be watching, finally warmed up to the idea that their daughter was a comedian. As Margaret explains, "My father called me and said, 'Welcome back to the family. You have proven yourself very well.'" Her father, who now lives in Korea, told her about the time that she was the topic of a radio talk show there. "They were basically having an open dialogue about me for about an hour." The radio show took phone calls and featured pieces of her performance on the Armed Forces network. "Because of that," she says, "I feel very well-known in Korea." Margaret's parents are now very supportive, but they don't always understand Margaret's jokes.

Margaret often renders comic portrayals of family members in her routine. For example, she has one brother, who is five years younger than she is and a student at the University of California–Riverside. After describing him as a surfer-turned-born-again-Christian, she imitates his voice in perfect Valley Dude intonation, asking, "Margaret? Have you found God?"

But Margaret most often portrays her mother to hilarious effect. She says she is very close to her mother, despite their differences. She enjoys talking about her mother because "it's one of those universal things, frustrations with your parents," especially being "very Americanized but coming from a very traditional home," which she believes is something everyone can relate to.

Now Margaret's mother even tries to suggest material for her daughter's shows. Margaret imitates her mother's Korean accent as she pitches an idea: "'Maybe you can say dat I did, I put da ice tray in da refrigeratah and den I take out too soon and dey was a waddah! Das so funny!' I'm like, 'Thanks, Mom.'"

When Margaret makes fun of her mother's accent, she does not come across as racist, unlike other comedians, because she is talking about "specific people, rather than immigrants in general." But Margaret does encounter a certain degree of racism when she tours the country, and in her act she sometimes addresses what it's like to be a young woman of color. Of the time she stayed overnight in a bed-and-breakfast in a small Michigan town, she recalls, "They had a kitchen there and I was thrilled because I never get to cook anything, so I went and bought all these things and I asked the woman, the proprietor of the house, if there was anything I could cook with. And she said, 'Oh, do you need a wok?' And I said, 'Oh, yeah, and some thousand-year-old eggs if you've got them.'"

Of the Deep South, Margaret adds her own twist to the common saying "It's not the heat but the humidity." Of racism in the South, she says, "It's not the hate but the stupidity." But stereotypical attitudes about people of color are not limited to certain areas of the country. When she appeared on the prestigious talent show "Star Search" (albeit the "international" version because, as Margaret says, "I'm so very international"), one of the show's producers asked American-born Margaret, "Could you be . . . I don't know . . more Chinese?" Margaret protested, "But I'm Korean," and the producer said, "Whatever."

Misconceptions about Asian Americans aside, Margaret has managed to break through to the mainstream. She

When Margaret dropped out of college to pursue a full-time career as a comedian, her parents were horrified. It was "the worst thing you can do in an Asian family. That's just worse than suicide or standing on a water tower and killing lots of people. At least mass murder can be justified if you have some sort of a college degree." Today, her mother tries to help her write her jokes.

"All American Girl" tells the story of the Kim family, who, like Margaret's real parents, own a bookstore where Margaret works part-time. "In my opinion," Margaret says, "I've always had my own show. It just hasn't been on TV yet."

was made an honorary member of the Friars Club, a sort of comedian's fraternity, which counts among its members such comic legends as Milton Berle—also, incidentally, a fan of Margaret's work. She also won the 1993 American Comedy Award for Best Female Comedian and was *Rolling Stone*'s recent pick for Today's Hottest Comic.

In the fall of 1993 Margaret signed an exclusive acting contract with Walt Disney Studios. Walt Disney Television and Touchstone Television, in conjunction with Sandollar Productions, developed a pilot for a new series to star the comedian. The show was originally called "The Margaret Cho Show," but was later changed to "All American Girl." By May 1994 the show was picked up by the ABC network to air among its new fall offerings.

"All American Girl" is about the "fictional" Kim family, which owns a bookstore where Margaret works part-time. On the show Margaret has an older brother, Kenneth (played by B. D. Wong), and a younger brother, Eric (J. B. Quon). Her TV mom is played by Jodie Long, and her dad by Clyde Kusatsu. Asian American comic actress Amy Hill plays Margaret's grandmother. Production on the series began in July 1994, with a mix of Asian and non-Asian writers on staff.

With 13 episodes planned so far, the show will address generational and multicultural issues and also promises to be very funny. But mainly the show is a vehicle for Margaret's unique take on life. As Margaret says herself, "In my opinion, I've always had my own show. It just hasn't been on TV yet. And so now it will be."

With fame and stardom at her doorstep, Margaret's only "problem" now seems to be her weight, but she even manages to make light of that topic. In her stand-up routine, she recounts the way network producers suggested she lose ten pounds before shooting began for her series' pilot. It wasn't so much that they asked her to lose weight, she explained, "but that they actually called a meeting about it."

Describing the way the meeting probably went, with network executives seated at a long boardroom table, and a big screen at the front of the room featuring a diagram of Margaret, she mimics a network exec wielding a pointer at various parts of her body and saying, "These are the problem areas we need to address. . . ."

But Margaret takes all aspects of show business in stride. She predicts that she will have an ego bigger than Roseanne's and Tom Arnold's combined. "I can't wait to get to the point where I can fire everyone in the morning and rehire them all after lunch."

Further Reading

Chan, Sucheng. *Asian Americans: An Interpretive History.*
Boston: Twayne, 1991.

Gee, Emma, ed. *Asian Women.* Berkeley: Asian American
Studies, University of California, 1971.

Golub, Caroline. *Immigrant Destinations.* Philadelphia:
Temple University Press, 1977.

Kitano, Harry H. L., and Roger Daniels. *Asian Americans:
Emerging Minorities.* Englewood Cliffs: Prentice Hall,
1988.

Perrin, Linda. *Coming to America: Immigrants from the Far East.*
New York: Delacorte, 1980.

Reimers, David M. *The Immigrant Experience.* New York:
Chelsea House, 1989.

Tachiki, Amy, ed. *Roots: An Asian American Reader.* Los
Angeles: UCLA Asian American Studies Center, 1971.

Takaki, Ronald. *From Different Shores: Perspectives on Race
and Ethnicity in America.* New York: Oxford University
Press, 1987.

Takaki, Ronald. *Strangers from a Different Shore: A History of Asian
Americans.* Boston: Little Brown, 1989.

Index

RONALD TAKAKI, the son of immigrant plantation laborers from Japan, graduated from the College of Wooster, Ohio, and earned his Ph.D. in history from the University of California at Berkeley, where he has served both as the chairperson and the graduate adviser of the Ethnic Studies program. Professor Takaki has lectured widely on issues relating to ethnic studies and multiculturalism in the United States, Japan, and the former Soviet Union and has won several important awards for his teaching efforts. He is the author of six books, including the highly acclaimed *Strangers from a Different Shore: A History of Asian Americans,* and the recently published *A Different Mirror: A History of Multicultural America.*

GERALDINE GAN is feature editor of *A. Magazine,* a quarterly of news and feature articles about Asian American lifestyles. She is the 1994–95 recipient of the Van Lier writing fellowship sponsored by the Asian American Writers Workshop of New York City. She is currently working on her first novel.